Best
Church Suppers

Gooseberry Patch

An imprint of Globe Pequot
246 Goose Lane
Guilford, CT 06437

www.gooseberrypatch.com
1•800•854•6673

Do you have a tried & true recipe...

tip, craft or memory that you'd like to see featured in
a **Gooseberry Patch** cookbook? Visit our website at
www.gooseberrypatch.com and follow the
easy steps to submit your favorite family recipe.
Or send them to us at:

Gooseberry Patch
PO Box 812
Columbus, OH 43216-0812

Don't forget to include the number of servings your recipe makes,
plus your name, address, phone number and email address. If we
select your recipe, your name will appear right along with it...
and you'll receive a **FREE** copy of the book!

Contents

Dedication

To everyone who knows that
the most delicious home-cooked
food can be found at church
potlucks, socials and
carry-in dinners.

Sunrise
Breakfasts

Barbara's Open-House Waffles

Barbara McCurry
Carpinteria, CA

*Every Saturday morning, I serve these for family & friends...
it's fun, and the neighbors love it! The millet flour can be usually
found in the same aisle as regular flour for baking.*

3 c. biscuit baking mix
1 c. whole-grain millet flour
1/8 t. baking soda
1/4 c. canola oil
3 eggs, beaten

3 c. buttermilk
2 T. water
Garnish: maple syrup,
  fresh strawberries,
  whipped cream

In a bowl, whisk together baking mix, flour and baking soda. Add
remaining ingredients except garnish and mix well. Drop batter by
1/2 cupfuls onto a preheated waffle iron; cook according to manufacturer's
directions. Top with maple syrup, strawberries and whipped cream.
Serves 6 to 8.

Welcome your neighbors for breakfast or brunch with steaming mugs
of coffee and frosty glasses of juice or milk. Serve morning favorites
buffet-style...what a fun way to enjoy each other's company!

Barbara's Open-House Waffles

Apple & Spice Baked French Toast

Apple & Spice Baked French Toast

Andrea Beck
Boise, ID

French toast with a twist...yum! Put it together the night before, then bake and serve in the morning.

1 loaf French bread, sliced
8 eggs
3-1/2 c. milk
1 c. sugar, divided
1 T. vanilla extract
6 to 8 apples, peeled, cored and
   sliced

1 T. cinnamon
1 t. nutmeg
2 T. butter, diced
Garnish: warm maple syrup

Place bread in a greased 13"x9" baking pan; set aside. Beat eggs, milk, 1/2 cup sugar and vanilla together; pour half of mixture over bread. Layer apples over bread; pour remaining egg mixture over the top. Set aside. Combine remaining sugar, cinnamon and nutmeg; sprinkle over apples. Dot with butter; cover and refrigerate overnight. Bake, uncovered, at 350 degrees for one hour, until lightly golden. Remove from oven; let stand for 5 to 10 minutes before serving. Slice into squares and serve with warm maple syrup. Serves 8 to 10.

9

When you're making pancakes for a crowd, keep them warm in a 200-degree oven. Just arrange pancakes on a baking sheet, set in the oven, then serve as needed.

Buttermilk Pancakes

Rita Morgan
Pueblo, CO

Sure, you could use a boxed mix, but this recipe is so simple and good. Perfect for our church's annual pancake supper! Serve with plenty of butter and maple syrup.

1-3/4 c. all-purpose flour
2 T. sugar
2 t. baking powder
1 t. baking soda
1/2 t. salt

2 eggs, beaten
2 c. buttermilk
1/4 c. oil
1/2 t. vanilla extract

In a large bowl, combine flour, sugar, baking powder, baking soda and salt; mix well and set aside. Combine eggs, buttermilk, oil and vanilla in a separate bowl. Whisk together and stir into flour mixture, just until moistened. Pour batter by 1/4 cupfuls onto a greased hot griddle. Cook until golden on the bottom. Turn pancakes when bubbles appear on the surface; cook until golden on the other side. Serves 6.

Fruity Pancake Topping

Tori Willis
Champaign, IL

Try this fruity sauce spooned over pancakes, waffles or French toast.

1/2 c. brown sugar, packed
10-oz. pkg. frozen raspberries,
  thawed

2 bananas, sliced
8-oz. can pineapple chunks,
  drained

Combine all ingredients in a blender; process until blended and smooth. Transfer to a saucepan; simmer over low heat until heated through. Makes about 3 cups.

Buttermilk Pancakes

Yummy Brunch Strata

Yummy Brunch Strata

Lynn Williams
Muncie, IN

All you need to accompany this feed-a-crowd dish is a tray of sweet rolls, a big pot of hot coffee and good fellowship!

1/3 c. oil
2 c. cooked ham, diced
3 c. sliced mushrooms
3 c. zucchini, diced
1-1/2 c. onion, diced
1-1/2 c. green, red or yellow
   pepper, diced
2 cloves garlic, minced

2 8-oz. pkgs. cream cheese,
   softened
1/2 c. half-and-half
1 doz. eggs, beaten
4 c. day-old bread, cubed
3 c. shredded Cheddar cheese
salt and pepper to taste

Heat oil in a large skillet over medium-high heat. Add ham, vegetables and garlic. Sauté for 3 to 5 minutes, until tender. Drain; set aside. Combine cream cheese and half-and-half in a large bowl; beat with an electric mixer on medium speed until smooth. Stir in vegetable mixture and remaining ingredients; blend lightly. Divide between 2 greased 11"x7" baking pans. Bake, uncovered, at 350 degrees for 35 to 40 minutes, until a knife tip inserted near the center comes out clean. Let stand 10 minutes; cut into squares. Serves 16.

13

Table tents let everyone know what goodies await in potluck dishes!
Fold an index card in half and jot down or rubber stamp the recipe
name on the front...a list of ingredients would be appreciated too. Be
sure to add the cook's name.

Heat & Hold Scrambled Eggs

Judy Collins
Nashville, TN

Serve with a stack of buttered toast and a platter of sizzling sausage links...yum!

1 doz. eggs, beaten	2 T. all-purpose flour
1-1/3 c. milk	1 T. pimentos, chopped
1 t. salt	1 T. fresh parsley, chopped
1/8 t. pepper	1/4 c. butter

Combine all ingredients except butter in a large bowl. Whisk until smooth and set aside. Melt butter in a large skillet over low heat; pour egg mixture into skillet. Cook and stir until eggs are set to desired consistency. May be held for up to one hour in a chafing dish or an electric skillet set at 200 degrees. Serves 6.

14

Mom's Cheese Grits

Elizabeth Smithson
Cunningham, KY

Mom always served us this recipe for special breakfasts! It's been in the family for years, from her mom on down. Now I serve it for brunch with my church ladies...they always ask for the recipe.

2 eggs, beaten	1/2 c. butter, sliced
1/4 to 1/2 c. milk	2 c. shredded Cheddar cheese,
1 c. long-cooking grits, uncooked	divided
1 t. garlic, minced	

Combine eggs with enough milk to equal one cup; set aside. Cook grits according to package directions; remove from heat. Add garlic, butter and one cup cheese to grits; stir until butter and cheese melt. Stir in egg mixture. Pour into a greased 2-quart casserole dish; top with remaining cheese. Bake, uncovered, at 350 degrees for 20 minutes, or until hot and bubbly. Serves 7 to 8.

Heat & Hold Scrambled Eggs

Quick Strawberry Cream Danish

Quick Strawberry Cream Danish

*Beth Bundy
Long Prairie, MN*

These are super easy, super tasty and super pretty. A couple of these with your coffee will definitely make your morning bright!

2 8-oz. pkgs. cream cheese,
  softened
1 egg, separated
1 t. vanilla extract
1 t. lemon juice

1 T. all-purpose flour
2 8-oz. tubes refrigerated
  crescent rolls
1/2 c. strawberry preserves,
  divided

Beat together cream cheese, egg yolk, vanilla, lemon juice and flour. Unroll and separate rolls; place a teaspoon of cream cheese mixture in the center of each triangle. Fold over edges of rolls, leaving center open. Brush with beaten egg white. Place on ungreased baking sheets. Bake at 350 degrees for 20 minutes. Remove from oven and cool slightly. Top each with a teaspoon of strawberry preserves. Makes 16.

17

You'll find colorful old-fashioned cut flowers like zinnias and dwarf sunflowers at farmers' markets. Arrange a generous bunch in a Mason jar and tie with jute for a bouquet that's perfect for a sunrise brunch... march several down the center of the tables!

7-Fruit Salad

Laurie Parks
Westerville, OH

The refreshing taste of this chilled fruit salad will be welcome during the heat of summer.

1/2 c. lime juice
1/2 c. water
1/2 c. sugar
2 nectarines, peeled, pitted and
 thinly sliced
1 banana, thinly sliced

1 pt. blueberries
1 pt. strawberries, hulled and sliced
1-1/2 c. watermelon, scooped into
 balls
1-1/2 c. seedless green grapes
1 kiwi, peeled and chopped

Whisk together lime juice, water and sugar in a bowl until sugar dissolves. Add nectarines and banana, stirring to coat; set aside. Combine remaining ingredients in a 2-1/2 quart glass serving bowl. Add nectarine mixture, gently tossing to mix. Cover and refrigerate for one hour. Serves 8 to 10.

Poppy Seed Mini Muffins

Donna Rasheed
Greer, SC

A basket of these little muffins is perfect for any breakfast or brunch occasion.

2 c. all-purpose flour
1 T. brown sugar, packed
1-1/2 t. baking powder
1/8 t. salt
1/4 c. butter, softened

8-oz. pkg. shredded Cheddar
 cheese
1 c. buttermilk
1 egg, beaten
2 to 3 T. poppy seed

In a large bowl, stir together flour, brown sugar, baking powder and salt. Cut in butter; stir in cheese. Add buttermilk and egg; stir just until moistened. Spoon batter into greased mini muffin cups, filling 1/2 full; sprinkle to taste with poppy seed. Bake at 400 degrees for 10 to 12 minutes, until tops are golden. Makes 3 dozen.

7-Fruit Salad

Southern Hashbrown Casserole

Southern Hashbrown Casserole

Sarah Crowder
McKinney, TX

*If you have never tried these potatoes, don't wait a minute longer.
This is my most-requested recipe at all of our Bible study potlucks...
I can never make enough!*

16-oz. container sour cream
10-3/4 oz. can cream of chicken
   soup
3/4 c. butter, melted and divided
1 t. salt
1 T. onion, minced

8-oz. pkg. shredded Cheddar
   cheese
32-oz. pkg. frozen southern diced
   potatoes, thawed and drained
2 c. corn flake cereal, crushed

Combine sour cream, soup and 1/2 cup butter in a large bowl; mix
well. Add salt, onion and cheese; blend in potatoes and stir well. Pour
mixture into a lightly greased shallow 2-quart casserole dish. Toss together
cereal and remaining butter; sprinkle over potatoes. Bake, uncovered, at
350 degrees for about 50 minutes, until golden and bubbly. Serves 8.

21

Help potluck hosts keep track of dishes by taping a label with
your name to the bottom of your casserole dish. Be sure to use
a waterproof marker!

Laura's Eggs Benedict

Laura Fuller
Fort Wayne, IN

You can easily substitute split biscuits for the English muffins and even sausage patties for the Canadian bacon...it's tasty either way.

4 English muffins, split and toasted
16 slices Canadian bacon
8 eggs
1/4 c. plus 1 T. butter, divided
1/4 c. all-purpose flour
1 t. paprika
1/8 t. nutmeg
2 c. milk
8-oz. pkg. shredded Swiss cheese
1/2 c. chicken broth
1 c. corn flake cereal, crushed

Arrange muffins split-side up in a lightly greased 13"x9" baking pan. Place 2 bacon slices on each muffin half. Fill a large skillet halfway with water; bring to just boiling. Break one egg into a dish; carefully slide into water. Repeat with 3 more eggs. Simmer, uncovered, 3 minutes or just until set. Remove eggs with a slotted spoon. Place one egg on each muffin half; set aside. Repeat with remaining eggs. In a saucepan over medium heat, melt 1/4 cup butter; stir in flour, paprika and nutmeg. Add milk; cook and stir until thick and bubbly. Stir in cheese until melted; add broth. Carefully spoon sauce over eggs. Melt remaining butter; stir in cereal and sprinkle over top. Cover and refrigerate overnight. Bake, uncovered, at 375 degrees for 20 to 25 minutes, until heated through. Serves 8.

22

Oven-Baked Pepper Bacon

John Alexander
New Britain, CT

Sure to be a hit at any breakfast or brunch!

1-1/2 lbs. sliced bacon
2-1/2 t. coarsely ground pepper

Arrange bacon slices in 2 ungreased 15"x10" jelly-roll pans. Sprinkle with pepper. Bake at 400 degrees for 25 minutes, switching pans between upper and lower racks halfway through. Remove bacon when crisply cooked. Drain on paper towels. Serves 12.

Laura's Eggs Benedict

Apple-Walnut Coffee Cake

Apple-Walnut Coffee Cake

Patty Sandness
Eastford, CT

Chopped apples and walnuts really set this coffee cake apart. It has all the yummy flavors of apple pie, but in a cake!

3 eggs, beaten
1 c. oil
2 c. sugar
1 T. vanilla extract
3 c. all-purpose flour
1 t. salt
1/2 t. baking powder

1 t. baking soda
3/4 t. nutmeg
1 T. cinnamon
2 c. Gala apples, peeled, cored and chopped
1 c. chopped walnuts

In a bowl, combine all ingredients except apples and nuts; mix well. Stir in apples and nuts; pour into a greased and floured Bundt® pan. Bake at 300 degrees for 45 minutes. Increase heat to 325 degrees and bake an additional 20 minutes. Cool on a wire rack for 20 minutes; turn out onto a serving plate. Drizzle with Glaze before serving. Serves 16.

25

Glaze:

1 c. powdered sugar
1-1/2 T. milk

1/2 t. vanilla

In a bowl, whisk together all ingredients to a drizzling consistency.

Cover the tube in a Bundt® pan with a small paper cup. When you pour in the batter, it won't spill down the center hole.

Maple-Pecan Brunch Ring

Leslie Williams
Americus, GA

A sweet & simple way to make a tasty treat for guests.

3/4 c. chopped pecans
1/2 c. brown sugar, packed
2 t. cinnamon
2 17.3-oz. tubes refrigerated
   jumbo flaky biscuits

2 T. butter, melted
1/2 c. maple syrup

Combine pecans, brown sugar and cinnamon; set aside. Split each biscuit horizontally. Brush half of the biscuits with melted butter and sprinkle with half the pecan mixture. Arrange topped biscuits in a circle on an ungreased baking sheet; overlap each biscuit slightly and keep within 2 inches of the edge of the baking sheet. Brush remaining biscuit halves with butter; sprinkle with remaining pecan mixture. Arrange a second ring just inside the first ring, overlapping edges. Bake at 350 degrees for 30 to 35 minutes, until golden. Remove to a wire rack; cool 10 minutes. Brush with maple syrup. Makes about 12 servings.

26

For light eaters at breakfast, add a tray of ready-to-eat fresh fruit and cheese cubes to nibble on.

Maple-Pecan Brunch Ring

Fresh Tomato Pie

Fresh Tomato Pie

Lynette Edmondson
Dickson, TN

*A delightful way to prepare sun-ripe tomatoes fresh from the
farmstand! Perfect for a summer brunch or luncheon.*

3 to 4 ripe tomatoes, diced
salt and pepper to taste
1/2 c. mayonnaise
1 c. shredded sharp Cheddar cheese

1 c. shredded Colby Jack cheese
1 T. dried chives
1 T. dried basil
9-inch pie crust, baked

Place tomatoes between paper towels to absorb some of the moisture.
Remove tomatoes to a bowl and season with salt and pepper. In a separate
bowl, combine mayonnaise, cheeses and herbs; gently fold in tomatoes.
Spoon tomato mixture into baked pie crust. Bake at 400 degrees for 20 to
30 minutes. Cool slightly before serving. Makes 8 servings.

Doughnut kabobs...a fun idea for a brunch buffet! Slide bite-size
doughnuts onto wooden skewers and stand the skewers in a tall vase
for easy serving.

Garden-Fresh Egg Casserole

Anne Muns
Scottsdale, AZ

Fresh tomatoes and spinach make this breakfast casserole extra special. I think it's perfect for overnight guests, or for carrying to an early morning breakfast social.

1-1/2 doz. eggs, beaten
1-1/2 c. shredded Monterey Jack
  cheese
1 c. buttermilk
1 c. cottage cheese

1 c. spinach, chopped
1 c. ripe tomatoes, chopped
1/2 c. onion, grated
1/2 c. butter, melted

Combine all ingredients in a large bowl; mix well. Transfer to a greased deep 13"x9" baking pan. Cover and refrigerate overnight. Bake, uncovered, at 350 degrees for 50 minutes to one hour. Serves 8 to 10.

Cheesy Mashed Potato Pancakes

Anne Ptacnik
Yuma, CO

A tasty way to use up leftover mashed potatoes. Fry them in a heavy cast-iron skillet to create crispy, cheesy edges that everyone will love!

3 c. mashed potatoes
3/4 c. shredded Cheddar cheese

salt and pepper to taste
1/4 c. butter, divided

In a bowl, combine mashed potatoes, cheese, salt and pepper; mix well. Form into flattened patties, using 1/3 to 1/2 cup potato mixture for each. In a skillet over medium heat, melt 1/2 to one tablespoon butter. Add several patties to skillet. Cook until crisp and golden; turn to cook other side. Add more butter to skillet for each batch. Serve warm. Makes 6 to 8 servings.

Serving an egg casserole at brunch? Please everyone by offering 2 versions...one with bacon or sausage, and one meatless dish with veggies and cheese.

Garden-Fresh Egg Casserole

Auntie Kay Kay's Sticky Buns

Auntie Kay Kay's Sticky Buns

Jen Sell
Farmington, MN

Everyone loves having my Auntie Kay Kay come to visit! She always starts making these sticky buns the day before so they are ready to bake the next morning.

2 16-oz. pkgs. frozen bread dough
1/2 c. cinnamon-sugar
1/2 c. butter
1/2 c. vanilla ice cream
1/2 c. sugar
1/2 c. brown sugar, packed

Place frozen bread dough in a lightly greased 13"x9" baking pan. Cover pan with plastic wrap sprayed with non-stick vegetable spray. Thaw dough overnight in refrigerator. Remove thawed dough from pan and cut into bite-size pieces; roll each piece in cinnamon-sugar to coat. Arrange coated dough pieces in same pan; set aside. Melt butter, ice cream and sugars in a saucepan over medium-low heat; stir until smooth. Spoon butter mixture over coated dough pieces. Bake at 400 degrees for 20 minutes, until golden. Serves 6 to 8.

33

Send a "Special Delivery" breakfast to someone under the weather. Tuck a package of fresh-baked muffins in a basket, tie a ribbon around the handle, then stop by for a visit.

Sausage Strata Brunch

Shannon Reents
Loudonville, OH

The ladies at my church used to serve breakfast to churchgoers once in awhile. This is a recipe I made often. You can substitute chopped ham or bacon for the sausage, if you'd like.

2 T. butter, softened
16 slices white bread, divided and
   crusts trimmed
1-1/2 lbs. ground pork sausage,
   browned and drained
8 slices sharp Cheddar cheese

10 eggs, beaten
3 c. milk
1/2 t. dry mustard
1/2 t. salt
3/4 c. corn flake cereal, crushed
1/4 c. butter, melted

Spread butter over one side of 8 bread slices. Place slices, butter-side down, in a 13"x9" glass baking pan. Layer with sausage, cheese and remaining bread. In a bowl, combine eggs, milk, mustard and salt. Pour over bread. Cover and refrigerate for 8 hours to overnight. Remove from refrigerator 1-1/2 hours before baking; uncover. Toss cereal with butter; sprinkle over top. Bake, uncovered, at 350 degrees for one hour and 20 minutes. Let stand 10 minutes; cut into squares to serve. Serves 10 to 12.

34

For buffets or potlucks, roll up flatware ahead of time in colorful napkins and stack in a basket...or let the kids do it for you!

Sausage Strata Brunch

Raised Doughnuts

Raised Doughnuts

*Pam James
Delaware, OH*

Every Tuesday night while I was growing up, my grandmother would make this dough for homemade doughnuts. Even now, nothing compares to them.

2 c. boiling water
1/2 c. sugar
1 T. salt
2 T. shortening
2 envs. active dry yeast
2 eggs, beaten
7 c. all-purpose flour
oil for frying
Garnish: additional sugar for
    coating

Stir together water, sugar, salt and shortening in a large bowl; sprinkle yeast on top. Set aside; let cool to room temperature. Blend in eggs; gradually add flour. Cover and let rise until double in bulk. On a floured surface, roll out dough 1/2-inch thick; cut with a doughnut cutter. Cover doughnuts and let rise until double in bulk, about 1-1/2 hours. In a deep saucepan over medium-high heat, heat several inches of oil to 360 degrees. Fry doughnuts, a few at a time, until golden; drain. Spoon sugar into a paper bag; add doughnuts and shake to coat. Makes about 4 dozen.

Soul-Warming Hot Spiced Cider

*Tiffani Schulte
Wyandotte, MI*

I've been making this delicious, soul-warming brew ever since my teenagers were babies...for church coffee hours, homeroom mom teas, PTO events, baby showers and just for fun. It smells so good!

1 gal. apple cider or apple juice
1/2 to 3/4 c. brown sugar, packed
1 whole orange, unpeeled
15 to 20 whole cloves
2 to 3 4-inch cinnamon sticks

Pour cider into a slow cooker. Stir in desired amount of brown sugar. Stud orange with cloves; add to cider along with cinnamon sticks. Cover and cook on low setting for 2 to 3 hours, but do not boil. May be kept at serving temperature in slow cooker for several hours. Makes 16 servings.

Fresh Strawberry Bread
Mary Patenaude
Griswold, CT

Serve this delicious bread with a dab of homemade strawberry jam or cream cheese.

3 c. all-purpose flour
2 c. sugar
1-1/2 t. cinnamon
1 t. baking soda
1 t. salt

4 eggs, beaten
1 c. oil
2 c. strawberries, hulled and diced
Optional: 1-1/4 c. chopped nuts

In a bowl, combine flour, sugar, cinnamon, baking soda and salt. In a separate bowl, whisk together eggs and oil; fold in strawberries. Gradually add egg mixture to flour mixture; stir until just moistened. Add nuts, if using. Pour batter into 2 greased and floured 9"x5" loaf pans. Bake at 350 degrees for one hour. Makes 2 loaves.

Whip up a crock of honey butter to serve with warm pancakes and breakfast rolls. Simply combine one cup honey with one cup softened butter and one teaspoon vanilla extract.

Fresh Strawberry Bread

Savory Chicken Brunch Bake

Savory Chicken Brunch Bake

Angie Ellefson
Milton, WI

My mother-in-law gave me this recipe when my husband and I were first married. I began making it to share and soon everyone was asking for the recipe. It's still a favorite.

2 10-3/4 oz. cans cream of chicken soup
1 c. sour cream
pepper to taste
5 boneless, skinless chicken breasts, cooked and cut into bite-size pieces

2 sleeves round buttery crackers, finely crushed
1/2 c. butter, melted
2 T. poppy seed
1/4 t. garlic salt

Blend together soup and sour cream in a large bowl; season with pepper. Stir in chicken and set aside. Place cracker crumbs in a shallow bowl; stir in melted butter, poppy seed and garlic salt. Spoon half the cracker mixture into a greased 13"x9" baking pan. Layer on chicken mixture and top with remaining cracker mixture. Cover with aluminum foil and bake at 350 degrees for 30 minutes. Remove foil and bake an additional 10 minutes, until top is golden. Let stand for 10 minutes before serving. Serves 6 to 8.

41

Planning a midday brunch? Along with breakfast foods like baked eggs, coffee cake and cereal, offer a light, savory main dish or two for those who have already enjoyed breakfast.

Smoked Salmon Strata

Mary Muchowicz
Elk Grove Village, IL

This is a scrumptious brunch dish to share with good friends. It's really easy too, so you'll have more time to spend visiting.

3 to 4 onion bagels, halved
3-oz. pkg. cream cheese, softened
1 T. butter, softened
5-oz. pkg. smoked salmon, sliced
dill weed to taste
8-oz. pkg. shredded Italian-blend
   cheese, divided

1 doz. eggs, beaten
1 c. half-and-half
1/2 t. salt
1/4 t. pepper
2 T. Dijon mustard

Spread bagel halves with cream cheese; cut each half into 4 pieces. Spread butter in a 13"x9" baking pan. Arrange bagel pieces in pan, cream cheese-side up; top each with a small piece of salmon. Sprinkle with dill weed; sprinkle one cup shredded cheese over salmon layer. Beat eggs, half-and-half, salt, pepper and mustard together; pour over cheese layer. Sprinkle remaining cheese over top. Bake, uncovered, at 350 degrees for 20 to 30 minutes. Makes 10 to 12 servings.

A simple crockery bowl filled to the brim with ripe oranges or nectarines and other fresh fruit looks so cheery on the breakfast table. It's a great way to encourage healthy snacking too!

Smoked Salmon Strata

Swirled Coffee Cake

Swirled Coffee Cake

Carol Doiron
North Berwick, ME

Boxed mixes make this delicious coffee cake a breeze to prepare!

18-1/4 oz. pkg. yellow cake mix
5-1/4 oz. pkg. instant pistachio
   pudding mix
4 eggs, beaten
1 t. vanilla extract

1 c. water
1/2 c. oil
1/2 c. sugar
2 t. cinnamon
1/2 c. chopped walnuts

Combine dry cake mix and dry pudding mix in a large bowl; beat in eggs, vanilla, water and oil. Pour half of batter into a greased Bundt® pan; set aside. Mix together sugar, cinnamon and walnuts in a small bowl. Sprinkle half of sugar mixture over batter in pan; swirl in with a knife. Add remaining batter; swirl in remaining sugar mixture. Bake at 350 degrees for 50 minutes, or until a toothpick inserted in the center tests done. Cool in pan; remove to a serving platter. Makes 12 to 15 servings.

Christmas Brunch Coffee Punch

Jodi Spires
Centerville, OH

Christmas wouldn't be Christmas without this punch at our family celebrations! If you like iced coffee or cappuccino, you will love it. I host a ladies' Christmas brunch every year and it's always a big hit with the ladies too.

2 c. water
2 c. sugar
1/4 c. instant coffee granules
1/2 gal. milk

1/2 gal. chocolate ice cream,
   slightly softened
1/2 gal. vanilla ice cream, slightly
   softened

In a saucepan, bring water to a boil over high heat. Add sugar; stir to dissolve. Turn off heat. Add coffee; stir to dissolve completely. Cool; pour into a covered container and refrigerate for several hours to overnight. At serving time, pour cold coffee mixture into a large punch bowl. Add milk and ice cream; stir to combine. Stir punch occasionally as ice cream continues to melt. Serves 12 to 15.

Pecan Bites

Hope Davenport
Portland, TX

These sweet morsels don't even need any frosting!

1 c. brown sugar, packed
1/2 c. all-purpose flour
1 c. chopped pecans

2/3 c. butter, melted and cooled
  slightly
2 eggs, beaten

Combine sugar, flour and pecans in a large bowl; set aside. In a separate bowl, whisk together together butter and eggs; stir into flour mixture. Spoon batter into greased and floured mini muffin cups, filling 2/3 full. Bake at 350 degrees for 22 to 25 minutes, until golden. Cool on a wire rack. Makes about 1-1/2 dozen.

46

Keep the coffee hour no-fuss. Brew a pot of steaming coffee and pour it into a thermal carafe. Simple to set out along with cream, sugar and coffee mugs and treats that are easy to eat while standing.

Pecan Bites

Hosting an early-morning breakfast social? Plan a make-ahead menu of overnight sweet or savory breakfast casseroles and slow-cooker hot cereals. Add a platter of muffins or quick bread and brew up some hot coffee and tea...everyone can sit down together with a minimum of effort.

 Mmm...maple bacon! It's simple to do for a crowd. Separate a pound of thick-sliced bacon and place on a rimmed baking sheet. Bake at 400 degrees for 15 to 20 minutes. Brush bacon with 2 tablespoons of pure maple syrup and return to the oven for 3 to 5 minutes, until crisp and golden. Drain on paper towels.

 For a breakfast fruit salad, toss together ripe fruit like blueberries, strawberries and kiwi. Drizzle with a dressing made by whisking together 1/2 cup honey, 1/4 cup lime juice and one teaspoon lime zest, or top with dollops of vanilla yogurt.

 Looking for an unusual centerpiece for a prayer breakfast table? Prayer plants have beautifully veined leaves that come together like folded hands. Wrap each pot in a pretty napkin and tie with jute...done!

Soup & Sandwich Suppers

Shirl's Corn Chowder Soup

Shirl Parsons
Cape Carteret, NC

This is my own recipe that I created a few years ago. It has become well loved at our church suppers.

2 c. potatoes, peeled and cubed
2 T. butter
1 onion, chopped
2 c. cooked ham, diced

2 c. frozen corn
2 qts. 1% milk
salt and pepper to taste

Cover potatoes with water in a saucepan. Cook over medium-high heat until partially tender; drain. Meanwhile, melt butter in a large soup pot over medium heat. Add onion and ham; sauté until onion is golden. Add potatoes, frozen corn and milk; season with salt and pepper. Reduce heat to low. Cover and simmer for one hour, stirring occasionally; do not allow to boil. Makes 10 servings.

Soup suppers are a fuss-free way to get together with friends and neighbors. Each family brings a favorite soup to share, along with the recipe...you provide the bowls, spoons and a super-simple dessert like brownies. What a delicious way to try a variety of soups!

Shirl's Corn Chowder Soup

Erma Lee's Chicken Soup

Erma Lee's Chicken Soup

Shirley White
Gatesville, TX

*My family still requests this comforting soup at the
first sign of cold weather.*

3 14-1/2 oz. cans chicken broth
2/3 c. onion, diced
2/3 c. carrot, peeled and diced
2/3 c. celery, diced
2 10-3/4 oz. cans cream of
   mushroom soup

4 boneless, skinless chicken
   breasts, cooked and cubed
8-oz. pkg. pasteurized process
   cheese spread, cubed
1 c. shredded Cheddar cheese
1 c. cooked rice

Bring broth to a boil in a stockpot over medium heat. Add vegetables; cook
until tender, about 10 minutes. Stir in remaining ingredients. Simmer over
low heat, stirring occasionally, until cheeses melt and soup is heated
through, about 15 minutes. Serves 6 to 8.

53

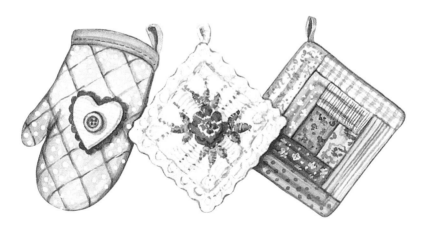

I plead for memories of olden times, and simple pleasures, and the
making of the most delightful music in the world, the laughter of
happy children...God bless us all and make us contented.
-A.M.Hopkins

Ruth's Champion Chili

Ruth Kaup
Springfield, MO

I won a chili cook-off with a milder version of this chili. For our church's latest cook-off, I knew I had to turn up the heat for the judges. I won! One lady shared that she had eaten two bowls full. The longer it cooks, the hotter it will become. A tablespoon of sour cream added to a bowlful will tame the heat, if preferred.

3 lbs. lean ground beef
2 onions, finely diced
2 stalks celery, finely diced
2 green peppers, finely diced
2 28-oz. cans diced tomatoes
2 40-oz. cans kidney beans,
　drained and rinsed
2 c. beef broth
10-oz. bottle steak sauce
6 T. chili powder

2 T. red pepper flakes
2 T. ground cumin
1 T. dried parsley
1 T. Worcestershire sauce
4 t. brown sugar
1 t. garlic powder
1 t. salt
6-oz. jar chopped jalapeño peppers
1 t. pepper

54

Brown beef, onions, celery and green peppers in a large skillet over medium-high heat. Drain; transfer to a 6-quart slow cooker. Add tomatoes with juice and remaining ingredients except jalapeños and pepper. Cover and cook on low setting for 5 hours. Add jalapeños and pepper; cover and cook for 2 more hours. Makes 12 servings.

Quickie Cornbread

Dawn Schlauderaff
Brooklyn Park, MN

A friend at work shared this 2-ingredient wonder with me.

8-1/2 oz. pkg. corn muffin mix   14-3/4 oz. can creamed corn

In a bowl, stir together corn muffin mix and creamed corn until moistened. Pour batter into an 8"x8" baking pan sprayed with non-stick vegetable spray. Bake at 400 degrees for 20 to 25 minutes, until set and golden. Cut into squares. Makes 8 servings.

Ruth's Champion Chili

Florentine Meatball Soup

Florentine Meatball Soup

Yvonne Van Brimmer
Apple Valley, CA

*This is a toss-together soup I came up with for a potluck at church.
It's a breeze to make in a slow cooker.*

14-oz. pkg. frozen Italian-style
  meatballs
16-oz. pkg. frozen green beans
16-oz. pkg. baby carrots
2 14-1/2 oz. cans sliced zucchini
  with Italian-style tomato sauce
2 14-1/2 oz. cans diced tomatoes
4 c. fresh baby spinach

1 T. Italian seasoning
1 T. granulated garlic, or more to
  taste
1 yellow onion, chopped
salt and pepper to taste
2 to 3 32-oz. containers beef broth
Garnish: grated Parmesan cheese

To a 6-quart slow cooker, add all ingredients except broth and garnish in
the order given. Do not drain zucchini or tomatoes. Add enough broth to fill
slow cooker 3/4 full. Stir to combine well. Cover and cook on low setting for
8 to 10 hours. Season with more salt and pepper, as desired. Ladle into
bowls; sprinkle with Parmesan cheese. Makes 6 to 8 servings.

57

Dress up bowls of tomato soup for a special luncheon...add a drizzle of
half-and-half and a sprinkle of chopped fresh basil.

Zesty Minestrone

Beth Hagopian
Huntsville, AL

*This hearty soup reheats well, so it's perfect to make ahead
for a soup supper.*

1 lb. Italian pork sausage links,
  sliced
2 t. oil
1 onion, chopped
1 green pepper, chopped
3 cloves garlic, chopped
28-oz. can whole tomatoes
2 potatoes, peeled and diced
4 c. beef broth
1/4 c. fresh parsley, chopped
2 t. dried oregano
1 t. dried basil
1 t. fennel seed
1/2 t. red pepper flakes
salt and pepper to taste
2 16-oz. cans kidney beans
1 c. elbow macaroni, uncooked

In a large saucepan over medium heat, sauté sausage in oil; drain. Add onion, green pepper and garlic; cook for 5 minutes. Add tomatoes with juice, potatoes, broth and seasonings; bring to a boil. Reduce heat to medium-low; simmer for 30 minutes, stirring occasionally. Stir in undrained beans and uncooked macaroni. Simmer for an additional 10 minutes, or until macaroni is tender. Makes 6 to 8 servings.

58

Herb Biscuit Knots

Gladys Kielar
Perrysburg, OH

Fantastic tasting and easy to make!

12-oz. tube refrigerated buttermilk
  biscuits
1/4 c. canola oil
1/2 t. garlic powder
1/2 t. Italian seasoning
1/8 t. salt

Cut each biscuit in half. Roll each piece into a 6-inch rope and tie in a loose knot. Place biscuits on a greased baking sheet. Bake at 400 degrees for about 9 to 11 minutes, until golden. Combine remaining ingredients in a small bowl. Immediately brush oil mixture over warm biscuits; brush again. Serve warm. Makes 20.

Zesty Minestrone

White Chicken Chili

White Chicken Chili

Andrea Pocreva
San Antonio, TX

*This chili recipe feeds a crowd! If you're hosting a smaller group,
it is easily halved.*

2 onions, chopped
1 T. olive oil
6 c. chicken broth
6 15-1/2 oz. cans Great Northern
   beans, drained and rinsed
3 5-oz. cans chicken, drained
2 4-oz. cans diced green chiles

2 t. ground cumin
1 t. garlic powder
1-1/2 t. dried oregano
1/4 t. white pepper
12-oz. container sour cream
3 c. shredded Monterey
   Jack cheese

In a large stockpot over medium heat, sauté onions in oil until tender.
Stir in remaining ingredients except sour cream and cheese. Simmer for
30 minutes, stirring frequently, until heated through. Shortly before serving
time, add sour cream and cheese. Stir until cheese is melted. Makes 16 to
20 servings.

61

Encourage table talk among dinner guests who don't know each other
well. Just write each person's name on both sides of the placecard,
where other guests can see it!

Shortcut Stromboli

Becky Kuchenbecker
Ravenna, OH

I have made this stromboli often for potlucks and family get-togethers, and I've gotten many requests for this quick & easy recipe! You can use different deli meats and cheeses for a delicious new taste every time.

16-oz. pkg. frozen bread dough, thawed
1 T. grated Parmesan cheese
2 eggs, separated
2 T. oil
1 t. dried parsley
1 t. dried oregano
1/2 t. garlic powder
1/2 lb. deli ham, sliced
1/4 lb. deli salami, sliced
1-1/2 c. shredded Cheddar cheese

Spread thawed dough into a rectangle on a greased baking sheet; set aside. Stir together Parmesan cheese, egg yolks, oil and seasonings in a bowl; spread mixture over dough. Layer ham and salami slices over dough; sprinkle with Cheddar cheese. Roll up jelly-roll style; place seam-side down on baking sheet. Let rise about 20 minutes. Brush with egg whites. Bake, uncovered, at 350 degrees for 30 to 40 minutes, until golden. Slice to serve. Serves 6.

A vintage covered soup tureen does double duty at a casual dinner of soup & sandwiches. It keeps the soup hot and tasty while also serving as a centerpiece.

Shortcut Stromboli

Bethany Wild Rice Soup

Bethany Wild Rice Soup

Susan Owens
Redlands, CA

Our church family always gathers in early December for a "Hanging of the Greens" night. It starts off with Christmas carols and a soup supper...my favorite is this wild rice soup.

2 c. wild rice, uncooked
2 T. butter
2 sweet onions, chopped
1/2 c. all-purpose flour
2 qts. chicken broth
6 c. cooked chicken breast, shredded

4 carrots, peeled and shredded
1/2 c. milk
2/3 c. blanched slivered almonds
1/4 c. fresh parsley, chopped
1/2 t. salt
1/2 t. pepper

Cover rice with water in a medium saucepan. Simmer over medium-low heat for 30 minutes. Drain; rinse rice and set aside. Meanwhile, melt butter in a large soup pot over medium heat. Add onions and cook until translucent. Stir in flour; mix well. Stir in broth, a little at a time; cook until slightly thickened. Add remaining ingredients and cooked rice. Reduce heat; simmer for 25 minutes. Makes 10 to 12 servings.

65

Katie's 8-Can Soup

Katie Majeske
Denver, PA

So easy and so good! The seasoning in the cans of chili is all you need to make this soup taste delicious. Add some crusty bread and your dinner is complete!

6 15-oz. cans assorted favorite vegetables

15-1/2 oz. can chili with beans
15-1/2 oz. can chili without beans

Combine all ingredients in a stockpot. Do not drain any of the cans. Cover and simmer over medium heat until heated through, stirring occasionally, 15 to 20 minutes. Makes 10 to 12 servings.

Sheila's Awesome Chicken Noodle Soup

Becky Holsinger
Belpre, OH

I got this recipe from a co-worker after she had brought this in for a luncheon. I loved it! When I took it to a church dinner, there weren't any leftovers to bring home. It really is the best chicken noodle soup I've ever had!

1-1/2 t. Italian seasoning
1-1/2 t. dried basil
1 t. garlic salt
1 t. salt
1 t. pepper
3 to 4 boneless, skinless chicken breasts, cubed
3/4 c. butter, divided

4 stalks celery, finely chopped
1/2 onion, finely chopped
1 c. baby carrots, finely chopped
48-oz. container chicken broth
12-oz. pkg. frozen egg noodles, uncooked
32-oz. container chicken broth, divided

Combine seasonings in a shallow bowl. Coat chicken cubes with seasonings; set aside. Melt 1/4 cup butter in a skillet over medium heat. Add chicken and cook until golden, stirring often. Transfer cooked chicken with pan drippings to a stockpot; add vegetables and large container of broth. Simmer over medium heat until vegetables are tender, about 15 minutes. Stir in frozen noodles and remaining butter. Simmer for 30 to 40 minutes, until noodles are cooked. As broth is absorbed by noodles, add remaining broth from small container as needed. Makes 8 servings.

Easiest-ever sandwiches for a soup supper...a big platter of cold cuts and cheese, a basket of fresh breads and a choice of condiments so guests can make their own. Don't forget the pickles!

Sheila's Awesome Chicken Noodle Soup

Dilly Egg Salad on Pumpernickel

Dilly Egg Salad on Pumpernickel

Jo Ann
Gooseberry Patch

The combination of Dijon, dill and red onion makes this lunchtime favorite extra special.

8 eggs, hard-boiled, peeled and
   diced
2 T. mayonnaise
2 T. Dijon mustard
1 t. dill weed

1/2 t. paprika
1/3 c. red onion, minced
salt and pepper to taste
8 slices pumpernickel bread
Optional: lettuce leaves

In a large bowl, combine all ingredients except bread; mash well with a fork or a wooden spoon. Serve egg mixture spread on bread or spooned onto lettuce leaves. Makes 4 servings.

69

If you're making sandwiches before a picnic, wrap them in wax paper and tie with a bit of kitchen twine. They'll look pretty on a platter... easy to grab & go too!

Cream of Broccoli Soup

Gloria Huff
Sandy Hook, VA

*This is our favorite Sunday lunch. As a church minister of music,
I am usually first to arrive at church and last to leave. A friend at a
previous church gave me this recipe, and it's a winter must in our
house! I have shared this recipe often.*

10-oz. pkg. frozen chopped
   broccoli
1 onion, chopped
1/2 c. water
12-oz. can evaporated milk
10-3/4 oz. can cream of mushroom
   soup

10-3/4 oz. can cream of celery
   soup
10-3/4 oz. can cream of chicken
   soup
salt and pepper to taste
Garnish: favorite shredded cheese

In a saucepan over medium-high heat, cook broccoli and onion in water
until onion is translucent. Do not drain. Transfer broccoli mixture to a
4-quart slow cooker; stir in evaporated milk, soups, salt and pepper. Cover
and cook on low setting for 3 to 4 hours. Add desired amount of cheese
before serving. Serves 6 to 8.

70

Parmesan Supper Bread

Sharon Crider
Junction City, KS

*With this recipe, it's oh-so easy to serve freshly baked bread
at dinnertime.*

1-1/2 c. buttermilk baking mix
1 T. sugar
1 T. dried minced onion
1/2 t. dried oregano

1 egg, beaten
1/4 c. milk
1/4 c. water
1/4 c. grated Parmesan cheese

In a bowl, combine all ingredients except cheese. Mix with a fork until soft
dough forms. Spread dough in a greased 8" round cake pan; sprinkle with
cheese. Bake at 400 degrees for 20 to 25 minutes, until golden. Cut into
wedges and serve warm. Makes 6 to 8 servings.

Cream of Broccoli Soup

Just Perfect Sloppy Joes

Just Perfect Sloppy Joes

Amy Wrightsel
Louisville, KY

*This recipe brings back memories of my aunt and me puttering
around together in the kitchen, trying to figure out how to make
these Joes just perfect.*

3 lbs. ground beef, browned and
   drained
1 onion, finely chopped
1 green pepper, chopped
28-oz. can tomato sauce
3/4 c. catsup

3 T. Worcestershire sauce
1 t. chili powder
1/2 t. garlic powder
1/2 t. pepper
8 sandwich buns, split

Combine all ingredients except buns in a 4 to 5-quart slow cooker; stir.
Cover and cook on low setting for 8 to 10 hours, or on high setting for 3 to
4 hours. Serve beef mixture spooned into sandwich buns. Serves 8.

73

Invite friends to bring along flower cuttings or divided bulbs from their
gardens to your next church picnic. Supply a few shovels, and in no
time at all you'll have a great beginning to a friendship garden.

Easy French Dip Sandwiches

Kathy White
Cato, NY

My husband is the pastor of our church and our family of ten regularly hosts meals with the congregation. These hearty sandwiches can feed a crowd!

4 lbs. stew beef, cubed
2 onions, halved
4 cloves garlic
2 10-1/2 oz. cans beef broth

4 c. water
4 t. beef bouillon granules
18 to 20 sandwich buns, split

Combine all ingredients except buns in a slow cooker; stir. Cover and cook on low setting for 8 to 10 hours. Remove beef to a bowl and shred, discarding onions and garlic. To serve, spoon beef mixture into sandwich buns. Ladle beef juices from slow cooker into small bowls for for dipping. Serves 18 to 20.

74

Warm sandwich buns for a crowd...easy! Fill a roaster with buns, cover with heavy-duty aluminum foil and cut several slits in the foil. Top with several dampened paper towels and tightly cover with more foil. Place in a 250-degree oven for 20 minutes. Rolls will be hot and steamy.

Easy French Dip Sandwiches

Lenten Mushroom-Barley Soup

Lenten Mushroom-Barley Soup

Mary Lou Thomas
Portland, ME

A warm and comforting soup for a chilly evening. Garnish with a dollop of sour cream.

2 14-oz. cans vegetable broth
2-1/2 c. plus 2 T. water, divided
3/4 c. quick-cooking barley, uncooked
1/2 c. onion, chopped
2 cloves garlic, minced
1 T. fresh basil, chopped

1/8 t. pepper
1/2 t. Worcestershire sauce
3 c. sliced mushrooms
1/2 c. carrot, peeled and shredded
2 T. cornstarch
Garnish: chopped fresh parsley

In a large saucepan over high heat, bring vegetable broth and 2-1/2 cups water to a boil. Stir in uncooked barley, onion, garlic, basil, pepper and Worcestershire sauce. Simmer for 5 minutes. Stir in mushrooms and carrot. Cover and simmer for about 5 minutes more, until barley is tender. In a small bowl, combine cornstarch and remaining water; stir into soup. Cook and stir until bubbly and slightly thickened. Cook and stir 2 minutes more. Serve individual bowls sprinkled with parsley. Makes 6 servings.

Keeping the menu all veggie? Round off a veggie main dish with special cheeses and breads...relax and enjoy.

Southern Pork Barbecue

Vicki Chavis
Fort Myers, FL

*Good-tasting barbecue isn't always smoked on a grill...
the slow cooker does the job just fine!*

3-lb. boneless pork loin roast,
   trimmed
1 c. water
18-oz. bottle barbecue sauce
2 T. Worcestershire sauce
1 to 2 T. hot pepper sauce

1/4 c. brown sugar, packed
1/2 t. salt
1 t. pepper
8 to 10 hamburger buns, split
Optional: deli coleslaw

Place roast in a 3-1/2- to 4-quart slow cooker; add water. Cover and cook on high setting for 5 to 7 hours, until tender. Shred roast; return to juices in slow cooker. Stir in sauces, sugar, salt and pepper. Cover and cook on low setting for one more hour. Serve pork mixture spooned onto buns; top with coleslaw, if desired. Serves 8 to 10.

Debbie's Foolproof Potato Soup

Candi Fisher
Gallipolis, OH

I never had good luck with potato soup...I always ended up with something more like mashed potatoes. My mother-in-law shared this recipe with me and it was a success!

8 potatoes, peeled and chopped
1/2 to 1 onion, diced
10-3/4 oz. can cream of celery
   soup

3 to 4 T. butter, sliced
1/2 c. shredded Cheddar cheese
1 T. garlic powder, or to taste
2 to 3 c. milk

Combine potatoes and onion in a large pot; add just enough water to cover. Bring to a boil over medium-high heat. Reduce heat to medium and simmer until vegetables are tender, about 15 to 20 minutes. Do not drain. Stir in soup; reduce heat and simmer for several minutes. Stir in butter, cheese and garlic powder; add milk to desired thickness. Cover and simmer over low heat for 15 to 20 minutes, stirring frequently. Serves 6.

Southern Pork Barbecue

Chicken Tortilla Soup

Chicken Tortilla Soup

Lynnette Zeigler
South Lake Tahoe, CA

Everyone loves this scrumptious Mexican-style soup. If you find you have an extra guest or two, stir in a can of black beans.

1 c. red onion, chopped
1 red pepper, chopped
2 cloves garlic, minced
2 boneless, skinless chicken
   breasts
1 T. oil
7 c. chicken broth

9-oz. pkg. frozen corn, thawed
1 t. ground cumin
2 c. tortilla chips, lightly crushed
1 c. shredded Cheddar cheese
Optional: sour cream, chopped
   fresh cilantro

In a Dutch oven, heat oil over medium heat. Add onion, red pepper and garlic; place chicken breasts on top. Sauté for 7 to 8 minutes, turning chicken once. Remove chicken to a plate; set aside. Add broth; bring to a simmer. Add corn and cumin; cook for 10 minutes. Shred chicken; stir into soup. To serve, place some chips in each bowl; ladle soup over chips. Sprinkle with cheese; stir gently. Garnish with dollops of sour cream and sprinkle with cilantro, if desired. Serves 6 to 8.

Cheddar & Green Pepper Cornbread

Darlene Fuller
Greenville, KY

One of our favorite comfort foods is cornbread. This dressed-up version is our favorite!

1 c. self-rising flour
1 c. cornmeal
1/4 t. onion salt
1 egg, beaten

1-1/2 c. milk
1 c. corn
1/2 c. green pepper, chopped
1 c. shredded Cheddar cheese

Combine flour, cornmeal, onion salt, egg and milk in a large bowl; stir until moistened. Stir in remaining ingredients; mix well. Spread in a lightly greased 13"x9" baking pan. Bake at 375 degrees for 30 minutes, or until golden. Serves 10 to 12.

Checkerboard
Cheese Sandwiches

Vickie
Gooseberry Patch

This cheesy filling can also be enjoyed as a dip with fresh veggies and crackers.

2-1/2 c. shredded extra-sharp
  Cheddar cheese
2-1/2 c. shredded Swiss cheese
1-1/4 c. mayonnaise
4-oz. jar diced pimentos, drained
1 t. dried minced onion
1/4 t. pepper
20 thin slices white bread, crusts
  trimmed
20 thin slices wheat bread, crusts
  trimmed

In a large bowl, combine shredded cheeses, mayonnaise, pimentos, onion and pepper. Mix well; divide in half. Spread half of mixture on half of white bread slices; top with remaining half of white bread slices. Spread remaining mixture on half of wheat bread slices; top with remaining half of wheat bread slices. Cut each sandwich into 4 squares. Arrange, stacked in pairs, on a serving plate in a checkerboard pattern, alternating white and wheat. Makes 40 mini sandwiches.

82

Turn pressed-glass jelly jars or pint-size Mason jars into charming votive holders. Add coarse salt or white sand to each and nestle a votive candle inside.

Checkerboard Cheese Sandwiches

Tangy Turkey Salad Croissants

Tangy Turkey Salad Croissants

Wendy Jacobs
Idaho Falls, ID

The day after Thanksgiving, my mom, my sisters and I decided we wanted more than just the usual turkey sandwich. We combined some of our favorite flavors and came up with these...we love them!

2 c. roast turkey breast, cubed
1 orange, peeled and chopped
1/2 c. cranberries, finely chopped
1/2 c. mayonnaise
1 t. mustard

1 t. sugar
1/2 t. salt
1/4 c. chopped pecans
6 croissants, split
Garnish: lettuce leaves

In a large bowl, combine turkey, orange, cranberries, mayonnaise, mustard, sugar and salt; mix gently. Cover and chill; stir in pecans just before serving. To serve, top each croissant half with 1/2 cup turkey mixture and a lettuce leaf. Top with remaining croissant half. Makes 6 sandwiches.

85

Make your ladies' luncheon a recipe swap! Invite friends to choose several of their best recipes to share, then make enough copies for everyone who will be coming. It's a fun way to pass along tried & true recipes, as well as enjoy a tasty lunch together.

Sausage Bean Gumbo

Jo Cline
Smithville, MO

Quick & easy...ready in 30 minutes! Super easy to double or even triple for a crowd.

14-oz. smoked pork sausage link, sliced
3   15 1/2-oz. cans Great Northern beans
14 1/2-oz. can diced tomatoes with sweet onions

1 stalk celery, diced
1/2 c. green pepper, diced
1/2 t. garlic powder
1/4 t. pepper
Optional: chopped fresh parsley or cilantro

In a soup over low heat, combine sausage, undrained beans, undrained tomatoes and remaining ingredients except optional garnish. Cover and simmer for about 30 minutes, stirring occasionally. Sprinkle servings with parsley or cilantro, if desired. Makes 4 to 6 servings.

86

To get the most slices from a round loaf of bread, first cut the loaf in half. Then place each half cut-side down on a cutting board and slice.

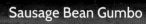
Sausage Bean Gumbo

Host a chili cook-off! Ask everyone to bring a pot of their "secret recipe" chili to share, then have a friendly judging for the best. You can even hand out wooden spoons, oven mitts and aprons as prizes.

 Kids are sure to know the old tale of Stone Soup...why not let it inspire a chilly-weather get-together? Invite everyone to bring a favorite veggie, while you provide a bubbling stockpot of broth or tomato juice. While the soup simmers, you can play board games, work on a service project or just chat for an old-fashioned good time.

Serve up bite-size sandwiches on slider buns or brown & serve rolls. Shredded pork, beef or chicken barbecue will go a lot farther...everyone can sample several, too.

White paper coffee filters are super for serving up sandwiches and wraps...no spills, no mess and easy for little hands to hold. Great for potato chips and popcorn too. Afterwards, just toss them away.

Bountiful Salads & Sides

Rainbow Pasta Salad

LaShelle Brown
Mulvane, KS

This is my husband's all-time favorite pasta salad. He requests it at all of our summer events. Add cubes of ham or salami for an even heartier salad.

4 c. rainbow rotini pasta, uncooked
1 cucumber, quartered lengthwise
   and sliced
1 tomato, chopped

4-oz. can sliced black olives,
   drained
1 c. ranch salad dressing
1/3 c. Italian salad dressing

Cook pasta according to package directions; drain and rinse with cold water. In a large salad bowl, combine cooked pasta, cucumber, tomato and olives; mix well. In a separate bowl, mix salad dressings together. Add to pasta mixture; toss to coat. Cover and refrigerate for at least one hour. Serves 8.

When it's just too hot to cook, how about a salad potluck? Try a chicken or tuna salad, a potato or pasta salad, a crisp green tossed salad and a fruity gelatin salad. Crusty bread and a simple dessert complete a tasty, light meal.

Rainbow Pasta Salad

Mandarin Orange Salad

Mandarin Orange Salad

Liz Plotnick-Snay
Gooseberry Patch

Quick & easy to prepare, this salad is delicious topped with a sweet dressing like Raspberry Vinaigrette.

4 c. green or red leaf lettuce, torn
   into bite-size pieces
2 15-oz. cans mandarin oranges,
   drained

1/2 c. walnut pieces, toasted
1/2 red onion, sliced

Combine all ingredients in a salad bowl. Just before serving, toss with desired amount of Raspberry Vinaigrette. Serves 4.

Raspberry Vinaigrette:

1/3 c. raspberry vinegar
1/3 c. seedless red raspberry jam
1 t. coriander or ground cumin

1/2 t. salt
1/4 t. pepper
3/4 c. olive oil

Combine all ingredients except olive oil in a blender. Process on high until blended; gradually add oil. Cover and chill.

93

Fruity gelatin salads are yummy topped with a dollop of creamy lemon mayonnaise. Stir 3 tablespoons each of lemon juice, light cream and powdered sugar into 1/2 cup mayonnaise. Garnish with curls of lemon zest, if you like.

Raspberry-Pretzel Salad

Gean Wilson
Greenwater, WA

A neighbor shared this recipe with me during a neighborhood barbecue. Now I take this dish along to any barbecue I attend... I'm always asked for the recipe!

1-1/2 c. pretzels, crushed
1/2 c. butter, melted
1 c. sugar, divided
8-oz. pkg. cream cheese, softened
8-oz. container frozen whipped
    topping, thawed

6-oz. pkg. raspberry gelatin mix
2 c. boiling water
2 10-oz. pkgs. frozen raspberries

Combine pretzels, melted butter and 1/2 cup sugar in a bowl; mix well. Press into the bottom of an ungreased 13"x9" baking pan to form a crust. Bake at 350 degrees for 5 to 7 minutes; let cool. Combine cream cheese, whipped topping and remaining sugar in a separate bowl; spread over baked crust. Cover and chill. Combine gelatin mix and boiling water in another bowl; stir well. Cover and chill until partially set. Stir frozen berries into gelatin; spread over cream cheese layer. Cover and refrigerate until serving time. Makes 12 to 15 servings.

Nestle serving bowls of chilled salads in larger bowls filled with crushed ice...sure to keep salads cool, crisp and refreshing.

Raspberry-Pretzel Salad

Corn Chip Salad

Corn Chip Salad

Rebekah Caillouet
West Milton, OH

I'm not sure where this recipe came from, but it has become a favorite for carry-ins. We even served it as part of the meal at my wedding!

1 head lettuce, shredded
6 to 8 eggs, hard-boiled, peeled
  and sliced
1-1/2 c. shredded Colby cheese

16-oz. pkg. bacon, crisply cooked
  and crumbled
4 to 6 c. corn chips, broken into
  smaller pieces

Combine all ingredients in a large serving bowl. Just before serving, add Mayonnaise Dressing to salad and toss. Makes 6 to 8 servings.

Mayonnaise Dressing:

1 c. mayonnaise
2 T. vinegar
1/4 c. milk

1/4 c. sugar
1/4 c. brown sugar, packed

Whisk together all ingredients until combined.

97

Crunchy Taco Coleslaw

Debie Pindral
Painesdale, MI

I always make this yummy coleslaw for potlucks and picnics... it's so simple to fix, yet everyone loves it.

16-oz. pkg. coleslaw mix
8-oz. pkg. shredded Mexican-blend
  cheese
1 to 2 tomatoes, chopped

16-oz. bottle western salad
  dressing
7-oz. pkg. nacho cheese tortilla
  chips, crushed

In a large salad bowl, toss together coleslaw, cheese, tomatoes and salad dressing to taste. Just before serving, stir in crushed chips. Makes 8 to 10 servings.

Loaded Potato Salad

Arden Regnier
East Moriches, NY

Our church's bake sales, held every Saturday in July, have expanded to salads, and we each have our own version of potato salad. One day I decided to make a salad with the flavors of a loaded baked potato... it became a big hit!

4 russet potatoes, peeled and cubed
1 t. salt
6 to 8 thick-cut slices bacon
1/2 c. mayonnaise
1/2 c. sour cream
1/2 c. shredded Cheddar cheese
1/4 c. fresh chives, chopped
salt and pepper to taste

Cover potatoes with cold water in a large saucepan; add salt. Cook over medium-high heat until fork-tender, 15 to 20 minutes. Drain; cool slightly and place in a large bowl. Meanwhile, in a skillet over medium heat, cook bacon until crisp. Drain on paper towels. In a small bowl, combine crumbled bacon and remaining ingredients, reserving some bacon, cheese or chives for garnish, if desired. Add to potatoes; mix well. Serve immediately, or cover and chill. Serves 6 to 8.

98

Lori's Quick Potato Salad

Lori Simmons
Princeville, IL

If you want a quick and tasty cool side dish, this is it! I make a double batch for potlucks. Garnish with deviled eggs and sweet pickles, if you like.

1 lb. potatoes, peeled and quartered
1/4 c. mayonnaise
1 t. mustard
1/2 t. dried minced onion
1/4 t. salt

In a large saucepan, cover potatoes with water. Bring to a boil over medium-high heat. Cook until potatoes are tender, 15 to 20 minutes. Drain; place potatoes in a serving bowl and allow to cool. Stir in remaining ingredients. Cover and chill until serving time. Makes 4 to 6 servings.

Loaded Potato Salad

Corn Pudding

Corn Pudding

Diana Chaney
Olathe, KS

This old-fashioned dish is out of this world made with freshly picked corn!

9 ears sweet corn, husks removed	1/3 c. plus 1 T. butter, divided
4 eggs, beaten	2 T. sugar
1/2 c. half-and-half	2 T. all-purpose flour
1-1/2 t. baking powder	1/8 t. pepper

With a paring knife, cut off corn kernels into a bowl. Scrape remaining pulp and "milk" from cobs; corn should measure 3 to 4 cups total. Set aside. In a separate bowl, whisk together eggs, half-and-half and baking powder. Melt 1/3 cup butter in a large saucepan over low heat. Add sugar and flour; cook and stir until smooth. Remove from heat; gradually add egg mixture, whisking constantly until smooth. Stir in corn. Pour corn mixture into a greased one to 1-1/2 quart casserole dish. Bake, uncovered, at 350 degrees for 40 to 45 minutes, until set. Melt remaining butter and drizzle over pudding; season with pepper. Place dish 5-1/2 inches from broiler; broil for 2 minutes or until golden. Let stand 5 minutes before serving. Makes 6 to 8 servings.

101

Make a delicious buffet even more inviting...arrange inverted cake pans or bowls on the table to create different levels. Cover all with a tablecloth and set food platters on top.

Meatless Stuffed Peppers
Rhonda Reeder
Ellicott City, MD

*My pals from garden club rave about these delicious sweet peppers!
I've found that the peppers fit best in an oval slow cooker.*

2 c. cooked brown rice
3 ripe tomatoes, chopped
1 c. frozen corn, thawed
1 sweet onion, chopped
1/3 c. canned kidney beans,
  drained and rinsed
1/3 c. canned black beans, drained
  and rinsed
3/4 c. Monterey Jack cheese, cubed

4-1/4 oz. can chopped black olives,
  drained
3 cloves garlic, minced
1 t. salt
1/2 t. pepper
6 green, red or yellow peppers, tops
  removed
3/4 c. spaghetti sauce
1/2 c. water

In a large bowl, combine cooked rice, tomatoes, corn, onion and beans. Stir in cheese, olives, garlic, salt and pepper; spoon mixture into peppers. In a small bowl, combine spaghetti sauce and water. Spoon half of sauce mixture into an oval 6-quart slow cooker. Place stuffed peppers on top. Spoon remaining sauce over peppers. Cover and cook on low setting for 3-1/2 to 4 hours, until peppers are tender. Makes 6 servings.

102

Herbed Ripe Tomatoes
Sonia Daily
Rochester, MI

*An easy recipe that's wonderful with juicy homegrown tomatoes.
Perfect for a backyard barbecue side dish.*

8 ripe tomatoes, sliced
1/4 c. fresh parsley or cilantro,
  chopped
2 T. cider vinegar or tarragon
  vinegar

1/4 c. olive oil
2 T. mustard
1 clove garlic, crushed
1 t. salt
1/4 t. pepper

Arrange tomatoes in a shallow serving dish; set aside. Combine remaining ingredients in a covered jar; add lid and shake well to mix. Drizzle dressing mixture over tomatoes. Cover lightly; let stand at room temperature at least 20 minutes before serving. Makes 10 to 12 servings.

Meatless Stuffed Peppers

Grandma's Calico Baked Beans

Grandma's Calico Baked Beans

Julie Harris
Boiling Springs, SC

I have fond memories of helping my grandma make this delicious dish the night before a church potluck. She would tie one of her big aprons on me and roll up my sleeves, so I could help make the sauce. As a newlywed I now make this for my own family and our church potlucks, and I am always reminded of those special times helping Grandma in the kitchen.

1/2 lb. bacon, diced
1 lb. ground beef
1/2 c. onion, chopped
1 clove garlic, minced
1/2 c. brown sugar, packed
1/2 c. catsup
1/4 c. water
1 T. cider vinegar
1 t. salt
1 t. mustard
Optional: 1/8 t. smoke-flavored
    cooking sauce
21-oz. can pork & beans
16-oz. can kidney beans, drained
    and rinsed
16-oz. can Great Northern beans,
    drained and rinsed

In a large skillet, cook bacon over medium heat until crisp. Remove bacon to paper towels; discard drippings. In the same skillet, brown beef, onion and garlic; drain. In a large bowl, whisk together brown sugar, catsup, water, vinegar, salt, mustard and sauce, if using. Add beans, crumbled bacon and beef mixture; stir well. Spoon mixture into a greased 2-quart casserole dish. Bake, uncovered, at 325 degrees for 45 to 60 minutes, until beans are bubbly and as thick as desired. Makes 10 to 15 servings.

Thank you for the world so sweet,
Thank you for the food we eat.
Thank you for the birds that sing,
Thank you, God, for everything.
-Edith Rutter-Leatham

Creamy Bacon & Herb Succotash

Vickie
Gooseberry Patch

You'll love this deluxe version of an old harvest-time favorite...I do!

1/4 lb. bacon, chopped
1 onion, diced
10-oz. pkg. frozen lima beans
1/2 c. water
salt and pepper to taste

10-oz. pkg. frozen corn
1/2 c. whipping cream
11/2 t. fresh thyme, minced
Garnish: 2 t. fresh chives,
  snipped

Cook bacon until crisp in a Dutch oven over medium-high heat. Remove bacon, reserving 2 tablespoons drippings in Dutch oven. Add onion; sauté about 5 minutes, or until tender. Add beans, water, salt and pepper; bring to a boil. Reduce heat; cover and simmer 5 minutes. Stir in corn, whipping cream and thyme; return to a simmer. Cook until vegetables are tender, about 5 minutes. Toss with bacon and chives before serving. Serves 6.

Paper napkins that are anything but plain...just roll, slip in plastic tableware and tie up with a cheery gingham ribbon.

Creamy Bacon & Herb Succotash

Bowties & Blush

Bowties & Blush

Brooke Sottosanti
Brunswick, OH

*A delicious meatless dish that can be prepared in no time...
and you'll be proud to serve it!*

16-oz. pkg. bowtie pasta,
  uncooked
1 T. butter
1 onion, chopped
1 banana pepper, chopped
2 cloves garlic, chopped
1 T. all-purpose flour

3/4 c. milk
1/2 c. whipping cream
1/2 t. salt
1-1/4 c. spaghetti sauce
1/4 c. grated Parmesan cheese
1/4 c. fresh basil, chopped

Cook pasta according to package directions; drain. Meanwhile, melt butter over medium heat in a large skillet. Add onion, pepper and garlic; sauté until tender. Stir in flour. Gradually add milk, cream and salt to skillet; bring to a boil. Stir in spaghetti sauce; reduce heat to low and simmer for 10 minutes. Pour sauce mixture into a large serving bowl. Add cooked pasta; mix gently. Sprinkle with Parmesan cheese and basil; serve warm. Serves 8.

109

Quick & Easy Italian Slaw

April Garner
Independence, KY

*This recipe is great to make in the morning so it's ready at suppertime.
I like to use a yellow pepper in the summertime and a red pepper for
fall...it looks so pretty!*

16-oz. pkg. coleslaw mix
1 green, red or yellow pepper,
  chopped

light brown sugar to taste
8-oz. bottle zesty Italian salad
  dressing

In a salad bowl, combine coleslaw mix and pepper. Sprinkle lightly with brown sugar; drizzle with salad dressing and toss well. Cover and refrigerate for at least 30 minutes to allow flavors to blend. Serves 8.

Potluck Pasta Salad

Shirley Howie
Foxboro, MA

*This is one of my favorite salads to take to a gathering. It is quick &
easy to make, and can be made a day ahead. It is also very versatile,
as you can substitute chicken or ham for the tuna, or use peas instead
of broccoli. However you make it, it will be delicious.*

2 c. bowtie pasta or elbow
   macaroni, uncooked
12-oz. can white tuna in water,
   drained and flaked
1 c. light mayonnaise

1 c. broccoli flowerets
1 c. carrots, peeled and chopped
1 c. celery, sliced
1 t. dill weed
1/2 t. pepper

Cook pasta or macaroni according to package directions. Drain; rinse with
cold water and transfer to a large salad bowl. Add remaining ingredients
and mix gently. Cover and refrigerate several hours to overnight. Makes
8 servings.

Create a light and airy brunch table setting for a bridal or baby shower.
Shades of pink, robin's egg blue, sage green and buttery yellow pair up
nicely with crisp white tablecloths, napkins and dishes.

Potluck Pasta Salad

Homestyle Green Beans

Homestyle Green Beans

Nancy Wise
Little Rock, AR

This is a such a tasty way to serve fresh green beans...
perfect alongside a baked ham.

2 lbs. green beans, trimmed
2 c. water
1-1/4 t. salt, divided
1/3 c. butter
1-1/2 T. sugar

1 t. dried basil
1/2 t. garlic powder
1/4 t. pepper
2 c. cherry tomatoes, halved

Place beans in a Dutch oven; add water and one teaspoon salt. Bring to a boil over medium-high heat. Reduce heat to medium-low; cover and simmer for 15 minutes, or until tender. Drain beans; keep warm. Meanwhile, melt butter in a saucepan over medium heat. Stir in sugar, basil, garlic powder, remaining salt and pepper. Add tomatoes and cook, stirring gently, until heated through. Spoon tomato mixture over warm beans and toss gently. Serves 8.

Savory Yellow Snap Beans

Debbie Jurczyk
Gilbertville, MA

When I was first married 30 years ago, my mother-in-law taught me to prepare snap beans this way. My husband can make a meal of a huge plate of these delicious beans!

3 lbs. yellow snap beans, trimmed
   and snapped into bite-size
   pieces
1/4 c. butter, softened
1 t. seasoned salt

1/2 t. garlic powder
1/8 t. pepper
3/4 c. round buttery crackers,
   crushed

In a large saucepan, cover beans with water. Bring to a boil over medium heat. Simmer until tender, about 20 minutes. Drain; add butter and stir to coat. Toss together with remaining ingredients and serve immediately. Serves 6.

Savory Cheese & Bacon Potatoes

Carolen Collins
Kansas City, MO

These cheesy mashed potatoes are out of this world!

2-1/2 lbs. Yukon Gold potatoes, peeled and quartered
3 T. butter, softened
2-1/2 c. mixed shredded cheese blend such as Swiss, Italian or casserole style
1/2 to 3/4 c. milk, warmed

4 slices bacon, crisply cooked and crumbled
2 t. dried sage
salt and pepper to taste
Optional: additional shredded cheese

Cover potatoes with water in a large saucepan. Bring to a boil over medium-high heat; cook until tender, 15 to 18 minutes. Drain potatoes; place in a large bowl and mash. Blend in butter and cheese; stir in enough milk to make a creamy consistency. Stir in bacon and sage; add salt and pepper to taste. Sprinkle with additional cheese, if desired. Makes 8 servings.

Keep a few packages of frozen ravioli tucked in the freezer for a speedy carry-in dish anytime. Quickly cooked and topped with your favorite sauce, they're terrific as either a side dish or a meatless main.

Savory Cheese & Bacon Potatoes

Cashew Slaw

Cashew Slaw

Lori Comer
Kernersville, NC

A dear friend brought this salad to our Sunday School dinner after church...everyone there wanted the recipe! It's scrumptious and so simple to make.

16-oz. pkg. coleslaw mix
2 3-oz. pkgs. chicken-flavored
　　ramen noodles
1/2 c. sugar

1/3 c. vinegar
1/4 c. oil
1 c. cashew halves
1 c. sunflower seeds

Place coleslaw mix in a large salad bowl. Crush noodles and add to coleslaw, setting aside seasoning packets; toss to mix. In a small bowl, whisk together sugar, vinegar, oil and reserved seasoning; pour over coleslaw mixture. Toss again; cover and chill 2 hours. Do not chill overnight as the noodles will become soggy. At serving time, add cashew halves and sunflower seeds. Mix well and serve. Makes 10 to 12 servings.

Lidded clear glass canisters make great serving containers for fruit salads at picnics. They can show off the bright colors of the fruit and keep pesky bugs off too!

Fruit & Nut Chicken Salad

Phyl Broich Wessling
Garner, IA

I make a double batch of this salad every year for our church's salad luncheon. There are never any leftovers!

4 c. cooked or grilled chicken, diced
11-oz. can mandarin oranges, drained
1-1/2 c. seedless green grapes, halved
1 c. celery, sliced
2-oz. pkg. slivered almonds, lightly toasted

1 c. mayonnaise
1/4 c. sour cream
1/8 t. garlic powder
1/2 t. salt
1/8 t. pepper
Garnish: lettuce leaves

Combine chicken, oranges, grapes, celery and almonds in a large bowl. In another bowl, combine mayonnaise, sour cream and seasonings. Pour mayonnaise mixture over chicken mixture; stir carefully. Cover and chill until serving time. Serve scoops of salad on lettuce leaves. Makes 8 to 10 servings.

Mom's Tropical Salad

Bobbie Kendall
McDonough, GA

Great for any summer church picnic! My mother has been making this for 40 years.

1 c. mandarin oranges, drained
1 c. pineapple chunks, drained
1 c. mini marshmallows
1 c. sweetened flaked coconut

8-oz. container sour cream
Optional: halved maraschino cherries, chopped pecans

In a serving bowl, mix together all ingredients except cherries and pecans. Cover and refrigerate overnight. At serving time, top with maraschino cherries and pecans, if desired. Makes 10 servings.

Fruit & Nut Chicken Salad

Heavenly Onion Casserole

Heavenly Onion Casserole

Lynne Bishop
Antioch, TN

This was handed down to me from my mother who would always take it to our church dinners. The pastor would ask her to bring this special, flavorful dish. He liked the name she gave it, for it truly is heavenly!

3 T. butter
3 onions, sliced
8-oz. pkg. sliced mushrooms
1 c. shredded Swiss cheese
10-3/4 oz. can cream of
  mushroom soup

1 c. evaporated milk
2 t. soy sauce
6 to 8 slices French bread
6 to 8 slices deli Swiss cheese

Melt butter in a large skillet over medium heat. Add onions and mushrooms; cook until tender. Spread in a lightly greased 11"x7" baking pan; sprinkle with shredded cheese. Combine soup, milk and soy sauce; pour over cheese. Top with bread slices, then cheese slices. Cover and refrigerate for 4 hours, or overnight. Bake, loosely covered, at 375 degrees for 30 minutes. Uncover and bake for an additional 15 to 20 minutes, until heated through. Let stand for 5 minutes before serving. Serves 6 to 8.

121

Hand out plastic zipping bags filled with crayons, mini coloring books and stickers to little ones…they'll be happy creating crayon masterpieces while waiting for dinner or an activity to begin.

Famous Broccoli Casserole

Paul Gaulke
Newark, OH

This casserole recipe is tried & true...we can't imagine a potluck without it!

2 6.9-oz. pkgs. chicken-flavored rice vermicelli mix
16-oz. pkg. frozen chopped broccoli
10-oz. pkg. frozen chopped broccoli

2 10-3/4 oz. cans cream of chicken soup
1 lb. pasteurized process cheese spread, cubed

Cook both packages of rice mix according to package directions. Meanwhile, cook both packages of broccoli according to package directions. Drain; place broccoli in a 6-quart slow cooker. Add soup and cheese; mix well. Stir in cooked rice mix. Cover and cook on low setting for 3 to 4 hours, until hot and bubbly. Makes 16 servings.

122

Scalloped Corn

Judy Voster
Neenah, WI

My husband loves corn and whenever he's tired after a hard day on the job, I make this comforting dish. Add a good movie after dinner and soon he's feeling much better.

15-1/4 oz. can corn, drained
14-3/4 oz. can creamed corn
3/4 c. milk
1 egg, beaten
1 c. dry bread crumbs
1/2 c. onion, chopped

3 T. green pepper, chopped
salt and pepper to taste
4 slices bacon, crisply cooked and crumbled
2 T. butter, diced

Combine corn, creamed corn and milk; stir in egg. Add remaining ingredients except bacon and butter; pour into a lightly greased 1-1/2 quart casserole dish. Sprinkle with bacon; dot with butter. Bake, uncovered, at 350 degrees for 30 minutes, until golden. Serves 4 to 6.

Famous Broccoli Casserole

Yummy Veggie Bake

Yummy Veggie Bake

Linda Beaver
Irving, TX

This recipe will win over even veggie-haters! It's easy and fast to prepare too. This was a favorite for our cozy Wednesday night meals at my church, where I made some very close friends.

1/4 c. butter, divided
2 c. green beans, trimmed
1-1/2 c. carrots, peeled and cut into strips
3/4 c. green pepper, cut into 1-inch pieces
1 onion, thinly sliced

2 c. celery, chopped
2 T. cornstarch
1 T. sugar
1/2 t. salt
2-1/2 t. pepper
14-1/2 oz. can diced tomatoes

Melt one tablespoon butter and spread in a 3-quart casserole dish. Layer fresh vegetables in dish. Combine cornstarch, sugar, salt and pepper; sprinkle over vegetables. Pour tomatoes with juice over top; dot with remaining butter. Cover and bake at 350 degrees for one hour, or until vegetables are tender. Makes 8 to 10 servings.

125

Easy, breezy decorating ideas for a summertime church social. Fill kids' brightly colored sand pails with flowers and a sprinkle of sand... centerpieces in a snap!

Grandma's Baked Mac & Cheese

Rebecca LaMere
Yulee, FL

My grandma is famous for this recipe at her church...she's always asked to bring it for church suppers and luncheons.

2 16-oz. pkgs. jumbo elbow
   macaroni, uncooked
1-1/2 c. butter, divided
1 to 1-1/2 c. all-purpose flour
4 to 6 c. milk

1-1/2 lbs. pasteurized process
   cheese spread, cubed
16-oz. pkg. shredded sharp
   Cheddar cheese
1-1/2 c. dry bread crumbs

Cook macaroni according to package directions; drain. Transfer cooked macaroni to a very large bowl; set aside. Melt 3/4 cup butter in a large saucepan over medium heat; whisk in one cup flour. If sauce is thin, add more flour. Add 4 cups milk; whisk to blend well. If needed, add more milk. Add cheese spread; cook and stir until melted. Add shredded cheese; stir until melted. Pour cheese sauce over macaroni; mix well. Spread macaroni mixture in a lightly greased 15"x12" baking pan or several smaller pans. Melt remaining butter in a saucepan. Add bread crumbs; stir until butter is absorbed. Sprinkle crumb mixture over macaroni. Bake, uncovered, at 350 degrees for about 30 minutes, until bubbly and golden. Serves 25 to 30.

Fix hot dogs for a crowd, the easy way! Fill a slow cooker with as many hot dogs as will fit, stood on end. Cover and cook on on high setting for 2 hours, or low setting for 4 hours. Uncover to serve hot...simple!

Grandma's Baked Mac & Cheese

For potluck success, make sure each dish has its own serving spoon, lifter or ladle. Cut any slice & serve dishes like lasagna into portions ahead of time.

 Most casseroles can be prepared the night before...just cover and refrigerate. Simply add 15 to 20 minutes to the original baking time. What a time-saver!

 Carrying a salad to a church potluck or a family get-together? Mix it up in a plastic zipping bag instead of a bowl, seal and set it on ice in a picnic cooler. No more worries about leaks or spills!

 Start a supper club with friends...choose a recipe theme each time, divide up the menu, then get together to cook and eat the meal. You'll have a ball and everyone will come away with some tasty new dinner ideas.

Main Dishes
to Share

Big Eddie's Rigatoni

Mary Beth Laporte
Escanaba, MI

This recipe was created by my 84-year-old father, who has always been a great cook and is affectionately called "Big Eddie" by family members. A delicious and satisfying meal when paired with salad and garlic bread.

16-oz. pkg. rigatoni pasta,
   uncooked
1/8 t. salt
2 lbs. lean ground beef
1-1/2 oz. pkg. spaghetti sauce mix
45-oz. jar chunky tomato, garlic
   and onion pasta sauce

8 slices mozzarella cheese, divided
8 slices provolone cheese, divided
8-oz. container sour cream
Garnish: grated Parmesan cheese

Cook pasta according to package directions; drain, mix in salt and set aside. Meanwhile, brown beef in a large, deep skillet over medium heat; drain. Stir in spaghetti sauce mix and pasta sauce; heat through. In a greased 13"x9" baking pan, layer half of cooked pasta, 4 slices mozzarella cheese and 4 slices provolone cheese. Spread entire container of sour cream across top; add half of beef mixture. Repeat layering, except for sour cream, ending with remaining beef mixture. Garnish with Parmesan cheese. Bake, uncovered, at 350 degrees for 30 minutes, or until hot and bubbly. Serves 8.

The secret to perfectly cooked pasta is to use plenty of cooking water, kept at a rolling boil...about a gallon per pound of pasta, in a very large pot.

Big Eddie's Rigatoni

Family's Favorite Lasagna

Family's Favorite Lasagna

Jo Anne Hayon
Sheboygan, WI

My husband says this lasagna is the best! I've been making it ever since we were married in 1977.

1 lb. ground beef
1/2 c. onion, chopped
6-oz. can tomato paste
28-oz. can diced tomatoes
1-1/2 t. dried oregano
1-1/4 t. garlic powder
1 t. salt
3/4 t. pepper

8-oz. pkg. lasagna noodles, cooked
8-oz. pkg. shredded mozzarella cheese
12-oz. container cottage cheese
Garnish: grated Parmesan cheese

Brown beef and onion in a large skillet over medium heat; drain. Add tomato paste, tomatoes with juice and seasonings; reduce heat and simmer for 20 minutes. In a greased 11"x7" baking pan, layer half each of lasagna noodles, mozzarella cheese, cottage cheese and meat sauce. Repeat layers, ending with sauce; sprinkle with Parmesan cheese. Bake, uncovered, at 350 degrees for 30 minutes. Let stand several minutes; cut into squares to serve. Makes 6 to 8 servings.

133

Cook lasagna noodles just until tender, then pull them, one at a time, from the water with tongs and place flat on a clean tea towel. The cooled noodles will be much easier to handle when layered with sauce and cheese. Now, that's using your noodle!

Chicken & Spaghetti Casserole

Nadine Rush
London, KY

Our church's hot food ministry cooks and delivers dinner to 50 people every Friday evening. This is the recipe I fix whenever we've decided on a spaghetti casserole...it feeds a crowd, yet it's not difficult to make. My daughters love it too.

5 to 6 boneless, skinless chicken breasts
2 to 3 stalks celery, diced
1 onion, diced
salt and pepper to taste
16-oz. pkg. spaghetti, broken in half and uncooked
2 10-3/4 oz. cans cream of chicken soup
8 slices pasteurized process cheese spread
10-oz. pkg. shredded mozzarella cheese

In a large soup pot, combine chicken breasts, celery, onion, salt and pepper; cover with water. Bring to a boil over medium-high heat. Reduce heat to low; simmer until chicken is tender, 30 to 45 minutes. Remove chicken breasts to a plate, reserving broth, celery and onion in soup pot. Bring broth mixture to a boil. Add spaghetti and cook until tender, 8 to 10 minutes; drain. Meanwhile, shred chicken. Combine chicken and soup in a large bowl; transfer to a greased deep 13"x9" glass baking pan. Spoon spaghetti mixture over chicken mixture. Arrange cheese slices on top; sprinkle with shredded cheese. Bake, uncovered, at 350 degrees for 25 minutes, or just until cheese melts and turns golden. Serves 12.

Whip up a side dish in no time at all...layer thick slices of juicy ripe tomatoes with fresh mozzarella cheese, then drizzle with olive oil.

Chicken & Spaghetti Casserole

Mandy's Easy Cheesy Chicken Casserole

Mandy's Easy Cheesy Chicken Casserole

Mandy Wheeler
Ashland, KY

This is a recipe I created by combining several other recipes. My husband loves it and it's always a hit at potlucks and reunions.

16-oz. pkg. wide egg noodles, uncooked
3 to 4 chicken breasts, cooked and cubed
24-oz. container sour cream
2 10 3/4-oz cans cream of chicken soup
8-oz. pkg. shredded Cheddar cheese
8-oz. pkg. shredded mozzarella cheese
1 sleeve round buttery crackers, crushed
1/4 c. butter, melted
2 T. poppy seed

Cook noodles according to package directions, just until tender; drain and transfer to a large bowl. Add chicken, sour cream, soup and cheeses; mix gently and spoon into a lightly greased 13"x9" baking pan. Toss together cracker crumbs and butter; sprinkle over top. Sprinkle poppy seed over cracker crumbs. Bake, uncovered, at 350 degrees for 25 to 30 minutes, or until heated through and crackers are crisp and golden. Serves 8 to 10.

Homemade Turkey Pot Pie

Sarah Sullivan
Andrews, NC

This recipe has been in our family for years...a real treat.

1/3 c. butter	2/3 c. milk
1/3 c. onion, chopped	2-1/2 to 3 c. cooked turkey,
1/3 c. all-purpose flour	chopped
1/2 t. salt	10-oz. pkg. frozen peas and
1/4 t. pepper	carrots, thawed
1-3/4 c. turkey broth	2 9-inch pie crusts

Melt butter in a large saucepan over low heat. Stir in onion, flour, salt and pepper. Cook, stirring constantly, until mixture is bubbly; remove from heat. Stir in broth and milk. Heat to boiling, stirring constantly. Boil and stir one minute. Mix in turkey and peas and carrots; set aside. Roll out one pie crust and place in a 9"x9" baking pan. Pour turkey mixture into pan. Roll remaining crust into an 11-inch square; cut out vents with a small cookie cutter. Place crust over filling; turn edges under and crimp. Bake, uncovered, at 425 degrees for 35 minutes, or until golden. Serves 4 to 6.

At potlucks, it's a good idea to keep aluminum foil, plastic zipping bags and plastic wrap on hand for wrapping up leftovers, or for someone who may just want to take a sampler plate home!

Homemade Turkey Pot Pie

Alice's Reuben Casserole

Alice's Reuben Casserole

Chrys Pfahl
Bay Village, OH

My mom always took this to church suppers and people awaited its arrival eagerly. She never would share the recipe, but I've done so in her memory. Note that if there's caraway seed in the sauerkraut or the bread, you won't need to add any.

8 slices pumpernickel or rye bread, cubed and divided
14-1/2 oz. can sauerkraut, drained
12-oz. can corned beef, crumbled
1 c. sour cream
1 onion, finely chopped
1/2 t. dry mustard
Optional: 1 t. caraway seed, crushed

8-oz. pkg. shredded Monterey Jack cheese
8-oz. pkg. shredded Swiss cheese
1/2 c. butter, melted
Garnish: Thousand Island salad dressing

Spread half of bread cubes in a 13"x9" baking pan that has been sprayed with non-stick vegetable spray. Layer on sauerkraut and corned beef. Mix sour cream, onion, mustard and caraway seed, if using; spread over corned beef layer. Layer on cheeses. Sprinkle top with remaining bread cubes and drizzle with butter. Bake, covered, at 350 degrees for 30 minutes. Serve warm, with salad dressing on the side. Makes 9 to 12 servings.

141

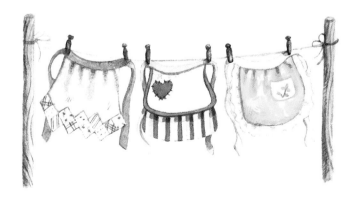

Keep hot foods hot, cold foods cold...don't let potluck food sit out longer than 2 hours, even if it still seems fine. Wrap and refrigerate any leftovers promptly. Better safe than sorry!

Baked Ham
Macaroni & Cheese

Julie Hutson
Callahan, FL

I simply love good old comfort food. This mac & cheese is very different from my traditional recipe, but it is spectacular! It has a creamy, cheesy texture with a little bit of spicy love from the pimentos and cayenne pepper. It makes a ton of pasta, so be prepared to feed a crowd or freeze half for later.

16-oz. pkg. penne pasta or elbow
    macaroni, uncooked
1/4 c. butter
1/2 c. all-purpose flour
4 c. milk
2 8-oz. pkgs. cream cheese,
    softened

1/2 t. cayenne pepper
16-oz. pkg. shredded Cheddar
    cheese, divided
2 c. cooked ham, diced
4-oz. jar chopped pimentos,
    drained

Cook pasta or macaroni according to package directions; drain and set aside. Meanwhile, melt butter in a large saucepan over medium heat. Whisk in flour; cook until lightly golden. Pour in milk, whisking constantly. Continue to cook until thickened and creamy. Add cream cheese, cayenne pepper and 3 cups Cheddar cheese to milk mixture; stir until cheeses are melted. Remove from heat. Combine cooked pasta, cheese mixture, ham and pimentos; transfer to a greased 3-quart casserole dish. Top with remaining Cheddar cheese. Bake, uncovered, at 375 degrees for 45 to 50 minutes, until hot and bubbly. Makes 8 to 10 servings.

Lots of different pasta shapes like bowties, seashells and corkscrew-shaped cavatappi work well in casseroles...why not give your favorite macaroni & cheese casserole a whole new look?

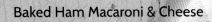

Baked Ham Macaroni & Cheese

Cheese-Stuffed Pasta Shells

Cheese-Stuffed Pasta Shells

Kathleen Sturm
Corona, CA

Filled with three kinds of cheese, these saucy shells are perfect for a special dinner...always welcome at potlucks too.

12-oz. pkg. jumbo pasta shells, uncooked
32-oz. container ricotta cheese
8-oz. pkg. shredded mozzarella cheese
1/2 c. grated Parmesan cheese
2 eggs, lightly beaten
1 T. fresh Italian parsley, chopped
1/2 t. salt
1/4 t. pepper
1/8 t. nutmeg
3 c. pasta sauce, divided
Garnish: additional mozzarella and Parmesan cheese

Cook pasta shells according to package directions; drain. Meanwhile, in a bowl, combine remaining ingredients except pasta sauce and garnish. Spread 1/2 cup pasta sauce in a greased 13"x9" baking pan; set aside. With a spoon, carefully fill each cooked shell with 1-1/2 tablespoons cheese filling. Arrange filled shells in baking pan, making layers of sauce and shells as needed. Pour remaining sauce over and around shells. Sprinkle with additional cheeses to taste. Cover tightly with aluminum foil. Bake at 375 degrees for 35 minutes, or until hot and bubbly. If made ahead and frozen, add a few minutes to the baking time. Makes 6 servings.

145

Making a pan of stuffed shells? Combine ingredients in a plastic zipping bag instead of a bowl. Blend by squeezing the bag, snip off a corner and pipe the filling into the shells...no muss, no fuss! Works great with manicotti too.

Best-Ever Garlic Bread

Vickie
Gooseberry Patch

A warm loaf of this irresistible garlic bread turns plain ol' spaghetti & meatballs into a feast! To save time, whip up the butter spread ahead of time and keep it in the fridge for up to two days.

3/4 c. butter, softened
6 T. mayonnaise
3/4 c. grated Parmesan cheese
2 T. fresh parsley, chopped

3 cloves garlic, minced
1/2 t. dried oregano
1 loaf French bread, halved
   lengthwise

In a small bowl, blend together all ingredients except bread. Spread butter mixture over cut sides of bread. Wrap bread in 2 pieces of aluminum foil; place cut-side up on a baking sheet. Bake at 375 degrees for 20 minutes. Unwrap bread and discard foil; place bread on a broiler pan. Broil until golden, about 2 minutes. Slice and serve warm. Makes one loaf.

146

Lighter-Than-Air Potato Rolls

Linda Cuellar
Riverside, CA

These are wonderful right out of the oven served with butter, jam, honey or apple butter.

1/2 c. instant potato flakes
1 t. sugar
2 T. butter, softened

1/2 c. hot water
1/3 c. cold water
2 c. biscuit baking mix

In a bowl, stir together potato flakes, sugar, butter and hot water. Stir in cold water and biscuit mix. Gently smooth dough into a ball on a floured surface; knead 8 to 10 times. On a floured surface, roll out dough into a 10-inch by 6-inch rectangle. Cut into 12 squares; arrange on an ungreased baking sheet. Bake at 450 degrees for about 10 minutes. Makes one dozen.

The supreme happiness of life
is the conviction that we are loved.
-Victor Hugo

Best-Ever Garlic Bread

Wild Rice Hot Dish

Wild Rice Hot Dish

June Sabatinos
Billings, MT

This dish is requested at every church social and there's never any left to take home! Serve piping hot or make up in advance, refrigerate and bake before serving.

2 lbs. ground beef
1/2 c. butter
1 lb. sliced mushrooms
1 c. onion, chopped
1/2 c. celery, chopped
2 c. sour cream

1/4 c. soy sauce
2 t. salt
1/4 t. pepper
2 c. long-grain and wild rice,
   cooked
1/2 c. slivered almonds

Brown beef in a skillet over medium heat. Remove beef from skillet; drain. Melt butter in skillet over medium heat; sauté mushrooms, onion and celery in melted butter 5 to 10 minutes, until tender. Combine sour cream, soy sauce, salt and pepper in a large bowl. Stir in beef, mushroom mixture, cooked rice and almonds. Place mixture in a greased 3-quart casserole dish. Bake, uncovered, at 350 degrees for one hour, or until heated through. Stir occasionally, adding a little water, if needed. Serves 12 to 16.

149

A roomy picnic basket makes light work of toting plates, silverware, napkins and cups to any potluck or carry-in.

Main Dishes to Share

Speedy Goulash

Laura Witham
Anchorage, AK

I love goulash! After some experimenting, I came up with what I believe is the easiest and tastiest recipe. I hope you'll agree!

8-oz. pkg. elbow macaroni,
  uncooked
1 lb. ground beef
1 onion
2 cloves garlic
1 T. paprika

1-1/2 t. ground coriander
1-1/2 t. ground cumin
1/4 t. nutmeg
14-1/2 oz. can diced tomatoes
3 T. sour cream
salt and pepper to taste

Cook macaroni according to package directions; drain. Meanwhile, brown beef in a large skillet over medium heat. While beef is cooking, grate onion and garlic directly into beef. Add spices and mix well. When beef is just cooked, drain. Add tomatoes with juice; warm through. Stir in sour cream, salt, pepper and cooked macaroni; serve immediately. Serves 6.

Feed-a-Crowd Pizza Casserole

Eileen Bennett
Jenison, MI

150

This dish feeds many hearty appetites and is that perfect bring-along dish for any potluck event.

8-oz. pkg. wide egg noodles,
  uncooked
1 lb. ground beef
1 clove garlic, minced
2 10-1/2 oz. cans pizza sauce

1-1/2 c. milk
1 c. shredded mozzarella cheese
1/2 c. sliced pepperoni
salt and pepper to taste
1/2 t. dried oregano

Cook noodles according to package directions, but for only 5 minutes; drain. Meanwhile, in a skillet over medium heat, brown beef with garlic; drain. In a large bowl, combine cooked noodles, beef mixture and remaining ingredients; mix well. Transfer to a lightly greased shallow 13"x9" baking pan. Bake, uncovered, at 350 degrees for one hour, or until hot and bubbly. If made ahead and refrigerated, bake for 1-1/2 hours. Makes 10 servings.

Speedy Goulash

Spaghetti Sauce for a Crowd

Spaghetti Sauce for a Crowd

Kathie Lorenzini
Ignacio, CO

This is my daughter Kerrie's recipe...we think it's the best!

28-oz. can crushed tomatoes
15-oz. can tomato sauce
12-oz. can tomato paste
1/2 c. onion, chopped
2 cloves garlic, minced
3 T. sugar
1 t. dried basil

1 t. dried oregano
1/2 t. salt
20-oz. pkg. Italian pork sausages,
　browned, drained and sliced
2 16-oz. pkgs. spaghetti,
　cooked

Stir together all ingredients except sausages and spaghetti in a slow cooker. Add sausages; cover and cook on low setting for 8 hours. Serve sauce over cooked spaghetti. Serves 12 to 14.

153

Taking a juicy slow-cooker dish to a potluck? Set it in a towel-lined laundry basket...easy to carry and the towels will catch any drips.

Pasta Bake Florentine

Jenny Flake
Gilbert, AZ

Not only is this baked pasta delicious...the variety of vegetables makes it colorful and appealing as well.

16-oz. pkg. rotini pasta, uncooked
2 T. olive oil
1 onion, finely chopped
1/4 c. red pepper, chopped
1/2 c. sliced mushrooms
1 lb. ground beef
1/2 t. salt
1/4 t. garlic salt
1/4 t. pepper
2 26-oz. jars pasta sauce
1 c. marinated artichokes, drained
   and chopped
10-oz. pkg. frozen spinach, thawed
   and drained
8-oz. pkg. shredded mozzarella
   cheese

Cook pasta according to package directions, just until tender; drain. Meanwhile, heat olive oil in a Dutch oven over medium heat. Sauté onion, red pepper and mushrooms until tender, about 5 minutes. Stir in beef and seasonings. Cook until beef is browned, about 5 to 7 minutes; drain. Stir in pasta sauce, artichokes and spinach until well combined. Fold in cooked pasta. Transfer to a lightly greased 13"x9" baking pan; sprinkle with cheese. Bake, uncovered, at 350 degrees for 15 to 20 minutes, until heated through and cheese is melted. Serves 8.

154

The simplest centerpiece can be the most festive. Set 2 or 3 pillar candles on a white plate, then tuck shiny ornament balls, seashells or fresh flowers around the base to highlight the season.

Pasta Bake Florentine

Renae's Taco Bake

Renae's Taco Bake

Renae Scheiderer
Beallsville, OH

This recipe was shared with me the first Christmas after I was married. It's become a favorite quick & easy supper at our house!

3 c. elbow macaroni, uncooked
1 lb. ground beef
1-1/4 oz. pkg. taco seasoning mix
15-oz. can tomato sauce
8-oz. container sour cream

1 c. shredded Cheddar cheese, divided
1/4 c. grated Parmesan cheese
Garnish: chopped green onions

Cook macaroni according to package directions, just until tender; drain. Meanwhile, brown beef in a skillet over medium heat; drain. Stir in seasoning mix and tomato sauce. Bring to a boil. Remove skillet from heat and set aside. In a bowl, combine cooked macaroni, sour cream and 1/2 cup Cheddar cheese. Spoon macaroni mixture into a lightly greased 13"x9" baking pan. Top with beef mixture and remaining cheeses. Bake, uncovered, at 350 degrees for 30 minutes, or until hot and bubbly. Garnish with green onions. Serves 6.

157

Beefy Shellaroni

Peggy Market
Elida, OH

This is a much-requested dish for our church potlucks...it always disappears very quickly! Serve with warm garlic bread and a tasty salad for a satisfying meal.

16-oz. pkg. medium macaroni shells, uncooked
2 lbs. ground beef

1 to 2 c. catsup
1 t. chili powder
salt and pepper to taste

Cook macaroni in a stockpot according to package instructions; drain. Rinse macaroni in a colander and return to stockpot. Meanwhile, brown beef in a large skillet over medium heat; drain. Add beef and remaining ingredients to cooked macaroni in stockpot; mix well. Cover and simmer over low heat for 15 minutes, stirring occasionally. Serves 8 to 10.

Meatloaf Mexicana

Jo Ann
Gooseberry Patch

Serve alongside zesty refried beans and a warm slice of cornbread.

1 lb. ground pork
3/4 lb. lean ground beef
1-1/4 c. shredded Monterey Jack
   cheese, divided
1 c. dry bread crumbs
1/2 c. taco sauce

2 eggs, beaten
1 T. fresh parsley, chopped
2 t. canned diced jalapeño peppers
1 t. salt
Garnish: chopped tomatoes, sliced
   green onions

Combine meats, one cup cheese and remaining ingredients except garnish in a large bowl. Gently press into a lightly greased 9"x5" loaf pan. Bake, uncovered, at 350 degrees for 55 to 60 minutes, until no longer pink in center. Top with remaining cheese; garnish as desired. Makes 6 servings.

Carol's Cheese Enchiladas

Carol Thompson
Casa Grande, AZ

158

This has become one of my children's favorite recipes. They requested it often when they were growing up. They never realized that I gradually tweaked it over the years to make it healthier!

8-oz. container low-fat sour cream
8-oz. pkg. low-fat cream cheese,
   softened
8-oz. pkg. low-fat shredded
   Cheddar cheese

1/2 c. onion, diced
4-oz. can chopped green chiles
10 8-inch flour tortillas
20-oz. can red or green enchilada
   sauce

In a large bowl, combine all ingredients except tortillas and enchilada sauce; mix well. Place 1/4 cup of mixture on the edge of each tortilla; roll up tightly. Spray a 13"x9" baking pan with non-stick vegetable spray. Arrange filled tortillas in pan, seam-side down. Spoon sauce over tortillas. Bake, covered, at 350 degrees for 25 to 30 minutes. Makes 10 servings.

Meatloaf Mexicana

Baked Maple Ham

Baked Maple Ham

Tina Wright
Atlanta, GA

Clove-studded ham makes a stately centerpiece for any meal. With any luck, there'll be plenty of leftover ham for sandwiches!

8- to 9-lb. fully cooked smoked
  shank ham, skin removed
1/2 c. whole cloves

1-1/4 c. brown sugar, packed
1/2 c. maple syrup

Score top of ham in a diamond pattern, making cuts 1/8-inch deep. Stud with whole cloves. Place ham fat-side up on a rack in a shallow roasting pan. Insert a meat thermometer into center of ham, making sure it does not touch bone or fat. Bake at 325 degrees for 2 to 2-1/2 hours, until thermometer reads 135 degrees. Combine brown sugar and maple syrup in a small bowl; stir well and brush over ham. Bake 20 to 30 more minutes, until thermometer reads 140 degrees. Remove ham to a serving platter; let stand 10 minutes before carving. Serves 16.

Delicious Baked Rotini

Megan Varvaris
Stewartstown, PA

This is a simple recipe that I created and that my family loves. It is very easy to prepare, makes enough to feed company and tastes delicious!

16-oz. pkg. rotini pasta, uncooked
1 lb. ground beef
45-oz. jar spaghetti sauce

8-oz. pkg. shredded Cheddar
  cheese, divided

Cook pasta according to package directions; drain. Meanwhile, brown beef in a large skillet over medium heat; drain. Combine cooked pasta, beef and spaghetti sauce. Spoon half of mixture into a 13"x9" baking pan sprayed with non-stick vegetable spray. Top with half of the Cheddar cheese; repeat layers. Cover with aluminum foil. Bake at 350 degrees for 30 minutes, or until hot, bubbly and cheese is melted. Makes 6 to 8 servings.

Whole turkeys and hams are a super bargain at holiday times. Make them the centerpiece of a sit-down meal, or slice and serve for scrumptious sandwiches.

Slow-Cooker Turkey Breast

Adrienne Kane
Chicago, IL

I always use my slow cooker to save space and time. I prepare the veggies and the butter blend the night before, then in the morning I just fill up the crock and turn it on.

1 to 2 onions, chopped
3 cloves garlic, pressed
1 c. chicken broth
1/4 c. butter, softened
3 T. fresh sage, chopped
3 T. fresh rosemary, chopped
3 T. fresh thyme, chopped
salt and pepper to taste
6-lb. turkey breast

Place onions and garlic in a 6-quart oval slow cooker; add broth and set aside. Blend butter, herbs and seasonings in a small bowl; rub mixture over turkey breast. Place turkey breast skin-side up in slow cooker. Cover and cook on low setting for 8 to 10 hours, or on high setting for 4 to 5 hours, until an instant-read meat thermometer reads 165 degrees. Remove turkey breast to a serving platter; let stand 10 minutes before carving. Serves 8 to 10.

162

Ziti Bake Supreme

Kristin Freeman
Dundas, MN

Always a hit when friends come for dinner!

16-oz. pkg. ziti pasta, uncooked
32-oz. jar spaghetti sauce
16-oz. container ricotta cheese
1/4 c. grated Parmesan cheese
2 c. shredded mozzarella cheese, divided

Cook pasta according to package directions; drain and return to stockpot. Stir sauce into cooked pasta. Spoon half of pasta mixture into a greased 13"x9" baking pan. In a bowl, combine ricotta cheese, Parmesan cheese and one cup mozzarella cheese. Spread all of cheese mixture over pasta mixture. Add remaining pasta mixture; top with remaining mozzarella cheese. Bake, uncovered, at 350 degrees for 30 to 40 minutes, until hot and bubbly. Makes 8 to 10 servings.

Slow-Cooker Turkey Breast

Sunday Meatball Skillet

Sunday Meatball Skillet

Doris Stegner
Delaware, OH

Oh-so delicious alongside roasted green beans and a bowl of homemade applesauce!

8-oz. pkg. medium egg noodles, uncooked
3/4 lb. ground beef
1 c. onion, grated
1/2 c. Italian-flavored dry bread crumbs
1 egg, beaten

1/4 c. catsup
1/4 t. pepper
2 c. beef broth
1/4 c. all-purpose flour
1/2 c. sour cream
Garnish: chopped fresh parsley

Cook noodles according to package directions; drain and set aside. Meanwhile, combine beef, onion, bread crumbs, egg, catsup and pepper in a large bowl. Mix well and shape into one-inch meatballs. Spray a large skillet with non-stick vegetable spray. Brown meatballs over medium heat, turning occasionally, until browned, about 10 minutes. Remove meatballs and let drain on paper towels. In a bowl, whisk together broth and flour; add to drippings in skillet. Cook and stir until mixture thickens, about 5 minutes. Stir in sour cream. Add cooked noodles and meatballs; toss to coat. Cook and stir until heated through, about 5 minutes. Garnish with parsley. Serves 4.

165

Fluffy mashed potatoes for a crowd will stay warm and tasty for hours...just spoon them into a slow cooker set on warm. Serve hot gravy from a smaller crock.

Famous Corn Chip Pie

Tiffani Schulte
Wyandotte, MI

I still remember the amazing lunch counter at Woolworth's dimestore. One of their best-known entrees was their Corn Chip Pie...a favorite I've recreated!

4 slices bacon, cut into 1-inch
   pieces
2 lbs. ground beef chuck
1 onion, diced
3 cloves garlic, minced
2 t. salt
1/4 c. chili powder, or less to taste
1 t. ground cumin

15-oz. can tomato sauce
6-oz. can tomato paste
3/4 c. water
14-oz. pkg. corn chips
8-oz. pkg. shredded sharp Cheddar
   or Monterey Jack cheese
Garnish: finely diced red onion,
   diced jalapeño peppers

In a large skillet over medium heat, cook bacon until crisp. Remove bacon to a plate and set aside, reserving drippings in skillet. Add beef, onion and garlic to skillet; cook until browned and drain. Stir in seasonings. Add tomato sauce, tomato paste and water to beef mixture. Simmer, stirring occasionally, for 10 to 20 minutes, until thickened. To serve, place a handful of corn chips in individual bowls. Spoon beef mixture and crumbled bacon over chips; sprinkle with cheese. Garnish with onion and jalapeño. Serves 6 to 8.

After a big dinner at church or home comes clean-up time. Keep vinegar handy in the kitchen for all your cleaning needs. It removes stains, sanitizes and is safe on just about any surface.

Famous Corn Chip Pie

Apple-Glazed Pork Chops

Apple-Glazed Pork Chops
Diane Cohen
Kennesaw, GA

Delicious and oh-so simple to fix.

4 pork loin chops
1/2 t. dried thyme
salt and pepper to taste
1 to 2 T. oil

1/2 c. apple jelly
1 T. Dijon mustard
1-1/2 T. butter

Season pork chops with thyme, salt and pepper; set aside. Heat oil in a large skillet over medium-high heat. Add pork chops; sauté until golden and cooked through. Remove pork chops to a plate; set aside. Add jelly to same skillet; cook until melted, scraping up any browned bits. Stir in mustard and butter; cook until bubbly and thickened. Return pork chops to skillet; turn to coat. Serve with sauce from skillet on the side. Makes 4 servings.

Onion-Baked Pork Chops
Shirley Howie
Foxboro, MA

This is a super easy recipe that I turn to when I want a quick and tasty dinner. Any leftover chops are good reheated. I like to cut up the leftovers into small pieces, mix with mustard and mayo, and spoon into pita bread to make a pocket sandwich. Delish!

2 eggs
1.35-oz. pkg. onion soup mix

1/2 c. dry bread crumbs
8 pork chops, 1/2 inch thick

Beat eggs in a bowl; combine soup mix with bread crumbs in a separate bowl. Dip pork chops into eggs; coat well with bread crumb mixture. Arrange chops in a greased shallow 13"x9" baking pan. Bake, uncovered, at 400 degrees for 40 minutes, or until chops are tender and cooked through. Makes 8 servings.

Shepherd's Pie

Kimberly Pfleiderer
Galion, OH

Stir in other favorite veggies if you like...corn and baby limas are tasty additions.

2 lbs. ground beef
1/2 onion, chopped
garlic powder and seasoning salt
   to taste
.75-oz. pkg. brown gravy mix
2 10-3/4 oz. cans cream of
   mushroom soup
2-1/2 c. water
1-1/2 c. frozen sliced carrots,
   thawed
10-oz. pkg. frozen peas, thawed
salt and pepper to taste
2-1/2 to 3 c. mashed potatoes
Garnish: paprika to taste

Brown beef and onion in a skillet over medium heat; drain. Season with garlic powder and seasoning salt; transfer to a large bowl. Stir in dry gravy mix, soup, water, carrots and peas; mix well. Spoon into a greased 9" deep-dish pie plate; sprinkle with salt and pepper. Spread mashed potatoes over top; bake at 350 degrees for 45 minutes, or until bubbly. Sprinkle with paprika. Makes 4 to 6 servings.

Don't limit your table coverings to tablecloths. Pick up a few yards of fabric that coordinates with your theme at the craft store. No hemming required...just tuck edges under!

Shepherd's Pie

Hosting a party for family & friends? Make it a potluck with a twist. You provide a hearty main course like spaghetti & meatballs, enchilada casserole or baked ham. Invite others to bring their own specialties like tossed salads, veggie dishes, hot rolls and so on. More fun and less work for everyone!

When you carry a lidded casserole to a potluck, use 2 large rubber bands to hold the lid on securely. Stretch a rubber band over the knob on the lid and pull over the handles on one side; repeat on the other side with a second rubber band.

Looking ahead to a big church homecoming or family reunion? Start planning early...3 months isn't too far in advance! Everyone will find it easier to reserve the date and you'll be a more relaxed hostess.

A wide roll of white freezer paper is handy for covering party and picnic tables. Before dinner, kids can have fun drawing on it with crayons...after dinner, just toss the paper or display their masterpieces!

Food for
Fellowship

Cari's Ranch Cheese Ball

Carilee Daniels
Newport, MI

One of my most-requested church potluck recipes! I have also changed it up a little by rolling the cheese ball in real bacon bits or seasoned dry bread crumbs. The flavor is best if made a day in advance, so it's a good make-ahead.

3 8-oz. pkgs. cream cheese, softened
2 1-oz. pkgs. ranch salad dressing mix
2 T. grated Parmesan cheese
2 T. Worcestershire sauce
1/2 c. onion, chopped
1/4 c. green pepper, diced
8-oz. pkg. shredded sharp Cheddar cheese
crackers, pretzels, chips or sliced vegetables

In a large bowl, combine cream cheese, salad dressing mix, Parmesan cheese, Worcestershire sauce, onion and green pepper. Use a potato masher or spoon to mix very well. Form cheese mixture into a ball; roll in shredded Cheddar cheese to coat. Wrap in plastic wrap; refrigerate for 24 hours. Let stand at room temperature about 15 to 20 minutes before serving. Serve with crackers, pretzels, chips or vegetables for dipping. Makes 15 to 20 servings.

Try serving "light" dippers with hearty full-flavored dips and spreads. Fresh veggies, baked tortilla chips and multi-grain crispbread are all sturdy enough to scoop up dips yet won't overshadow the flavor of the dip.

Cari's Ranch Cheese Ball

Pizza Roll Snacks

Pizza Roll Snacks

Diane Cohen
The Woodlands, TX

Who needs frozen pizza rolls when it's a snap to make these yummy rolls? My girls love them for after-school snacks. If there are any leftovers, they warm up great in the microwave.

8-oz. tube refrigerated crescent
  rolls
3 T. pizza sauce
1/4 c. grated Parmesan cheese

16 slices pepperoni, divided
1/3 c. shredded mozzarella cheese,
  divided
Garnish: small fresh basil leaves

Unroll crescent roll dough but do not separate; press perforations to seal. Spread pizza sauce evenly over dough, leaving a one-inch border. Sprinkle with Parmesan cheese and roll up, starting with the long side. Using a sharp knife, cut roll into 16 slices. Place slices cut-side down on a greased baking sheet. Top each slice with one pepperoni slice and one teaspoon mozzarella cheese. Bake at 375 degrees for 9 to 11 minutes, until edges are golden and cheese melts. Garnish with basil leaves. Makes 16.

Elsye's Mini Meat Turnovers

Malacha Payton
Edmond, OK

This party-pleaser was shared by a friend who passed away several years ago. I serve these often, and always have good memories of her.

1/2 lb. lean ground beef
1-oz. pkg. beef-onion or onion-
  mushroom soup mix
1/2 c. canned sliced water
  chestnuts, drained

1 c. canned bean sprouts, drained
2 T. onion, chopped
2 8-oz. tubes refrigerated crescent
  rolls

In a skillet over medium heat, combine all ingredients except crescent rolls. Brown beef well; drain. Separate crescent rolls and cut in half diagonally. Place a spoonful of mixture in the center of each triangle; fold over and seal edges. Arrange turnovers on an ungreased baking sheet. Bake at 375 degrees for 15 minutes, or until golden. Serve warm. Makes about 2-1/2 dozen.

Pepperoni Puffs

Marcia Marcoux
Charlton, MA

These tasty morsels are really easy to stir up and hard to resist...
you might want to make a double batch!

1 c. all-purpose flour
1 t. baking powder
1 c. milk
1 egg, beaten

1 c. shredded Cheddar cheese
1-1/2 c. pepperoni, diced
Garnish: warmed pizza sauce

Combine flour, baking powder, milk, egg and cheese in a bowl; mix well. Stir in pepperoni; let stand for 15 minutes. Spoon into greased mini muffin cups, filling 3/4 full. Bake at 350 degrees for 25 to 35 minutes, until golden. Serve with warmed pizza sauce for dipping. Makes 2 dozen.

A church social is a super time to have a Swap & Shop. Everyone brings along gently-used items they no longer need...then they can have fun swapping for items they want to take home!

Pepperoni Puffs

Artichoke-Garlic Dip

Artichoke-Garlic Dip

Carole Larkins
Elmendorf Air Force Base, AK

Serve this savory spread in a hollowed-out sourdough bread loaf, with chunks of bread and hearty crackers for dipping.

14-oz. can artichokes, drained and
   chopped
1/2 c. grated Parmesan cheese
8-oz. pkg. cream cheese, softened
1/2 c. mayonnaise

2 cloves garlic, minced
1/2 t. dill weed
Optional: additional Parmesan
   cheese

Combine artichokes, cheeses, mayonnaise, garlic and dill weed in an ungreased 10" pie plate. If desired, sprinkle with additional Parmesan cheese. Bake, uncovered, at 400 degrees for 15 minutes, or until golden. Garnish as desired. Makes about 3-1/2 cups.

Lightened-Up Spinach Dip

Patty Flak
Erie, PA

A healthy yet tasty version of an old favorite... there's no cream cheese in it.

10-oz. pkg. frozen chopped
   spinach, thawed and well
   drained
1/2 c. part-skim ricotta cheese
1/2 c. crumbled reduced-fat feta
   cheese

1/4 c. non-fat mayonnaise
1/4 c. fresh dill weed, snipped
2 green onions, chopped
1 to 2 t. prepared horseradish
1 t. lemon juice
cut-up vegetables, pita chips

In a serving bowl, combine all ingredients except vegetables and pita chips. Blend until smooth; cover and chill until serving time. Serve with vegetables and pita chips. Makes 12 servings.

Nacho Chicken Dip

Trudy Williams
Middlesex, NC

We love this delicious dip at parties...it's even good as a meal, paired with a side salad.

16-oz. can refried beans
12-oz. can chicken, drained and
  flaked
16-oz. jar chunky salsa

8-oz. pkg. shredded Mexican-blend
  cheese
tortilla chips

Layer beans, chicken, salsa and cheese in a lightly greased one-quart casserole dish. Bake, uncovered, at 350 degrees for 30 minutes, or until cheese is bubbly. Serve hot with tortilla chips. Makes about 6-1/2 cups.

Other things may change us,
but we start and end with family.
- Anthony Brandt

Nacho Chicken Dip

Pizza Fondue

Pizza Fondue

Michelle Golz
Freeport, IL

Keep this savory dip warm in a fondue pot or simmering on low in a slow cooker.

1 lb. ground beef
1 onion, chopped
2 10-oz. cans pizza sauce
1 T. cornstarch
1-1/2 t. fennel seed
1-1/2 t. dried oregano

1/4 t. garlic powder
2-1/2 c. shredded Cheddar cheese
2 c. shredded mozzarella cheese
2 loaves French bread, sliced and
    toasted

Brown beef and onion in a skillet over medium heat; drain. Add remaining ingredients except bread. Simmer over low heat, stirring occasionally, until cheese melts. Serve hot with bread slices for dipping. Serves 6 to 8.

Double Tomato Bruschetta

Penny Heins
Choctaw, OK

185

I take this delicious appetizer to share with our small group get-together at church.

1 French baguette loaf, sliced
    3/4-inch thick
6 roma tomatoes, chopped
1/2 c. sun-dried tomatoes, packed
    in oil
3 cloves garlic, minced

1/4 c. olive oil
2 t. balsamic vinegar
1/4 c. fresh basil, stems removed
1/4 t. salt
1/4 t. pepper

On a baking sheet, arrange baguette slices in a single layer; set aside. In a large bowl, combine remaining ingredients; let stand for 10 minutes. Broil baguette slices for one to 2 minutes, until lightly golden. Spoon tomato mixture evenly over baguette slices just before serving. Serves 6.

Dried Beef Cheese Ball

Sharon Hall
Delaware, OH

*My famous "secret ingredient" recipe for the yummiest
cheese ball ever!*

2 8-oz. pkgs. cream cheese,
   softened
1 c. shredded Cheddar cheese
2-1/2 oz. pkg. dried beef, finely
   chopped and divided
3 T. green onion, chopped

2 to 3 T. mayonnaise-style salad
   dressing
1 t. Worcestershire sauce
1/2 c. chopped walnuts
assorted snack crackers

Combine all ingredients except walnuts and crackers, setting aside 1/4 cup
chopped beef. Blend well and form into a ball. Mix nuts and reserved beef;
roll cheese ball in mixture to coat. Wrap in plastic wrap; chill 3 to 4 hours.
Serve with crackers. Makes one cheese ball.

186

When you need to chill lots of juice boxes, cans of soda pop or
bottles of water, you'll find they chill more quickly on ice than in the
refrigerator. Just add beverages to an ice-filled cooler or galvanized tub.
You'll save valuable refrigerator space too!

Dried Beef Cheese Ball

Pork & Apple Meatballs

Pork & Apple Meatballs

Emmaline Dunkley
Pine City, MN

Serve these yummy meatballs right away, or keep warm in a slow cooker until serving time.

1 lb. ground pork sausage
1-1/4 c. pork-flavored stuffing mix
1/2 c. low-sodium chicken broth
1/2 c. Honeycrisp apple, peeled, cored and diced
1/2 c. onion, diced

1 egg, beaten
1-1/2 t. mustard
1/2 c. shredded sharp Cheddar cheese
Optional: barbecue sauce

Combine all ingredients except barbecue sauce in a large bowl. Mix well; form into balls by tablespoonfuls. Place meatballs on a lightly greased 15"x10" jelly-roll pan. Bake at 350 degrees for 18 to 20 minutes, until meatballs are no longer pink in the middle. Brush with barbecue sauce, if desired. Serves 8 to 10.

189

On warm fall days, set up harvest tables and chairs outdoors for a fellowship supper. Decorate with plump pumpkins, bittersweet wreaths, straw bales and scarecrows.

Salmon Loaf Dip

Suzanne Morley
Kent, England

A real favorite at family gatherings! Friends can't stop eating it and always ask for the recipe.

1 large loaf crusty bread
1 onion, finely chopped
1 to 2 t. oil
8-oz. pkg. cream cheese, softened
2 7-3/4 oz. cans salmon, drained

3 to 4 T. sour cream
1 t. hot pepper sauce
1/8 t. salt
1/8 t. pepper
1 t. fresh dill weed, chopped

Slice the top from bread loaf. Hollow out the center; cut bread into cubes and aside. In a saucepan over medium heat, sauté onion in oil until tender; transfer onion to a bowl. Add remaining ingredients to onion; mix well. Spoon mixture into hollow loaf; replace top of loaf and place on an ungreased baking sheet. Bake at 350 degrees for 30 minutes. Add reserved bread cubes to baking sheet alongside loaf; continue baking for 3 to 5 more minutes. Serve dip with warmed bread cubes. Serves 4 to 8.

190

Aunt Rita's Shrimp Dip

Lori Williams
Acton, ME

Every time I make this recipe, I think of my Aunt Rita and my grandmother too! They were sisters-in-law and they had so much fun together. This recipe is so easy because all of the ingredients are staples. Whip it up whenever it's party time.

8-oz. pkg. cream cheese, softened
1 T. mayonnaise
1 t. catsup
1 t. mustard

1/2 c. celery, finely chopped
1/4 c. onion, finely chopped
4-1/4 oz. can tiny shrimp, drained
hearty crackers

In a bowl, blend together cream cheese, mayonnaise, catsup and mustard. Stir in celery and onion; gently fold in shrimp. Cover and chill for at least one hour. Serve with crackers. Serves 8.

Salmon Loaf Dip

Strawberry Fruit Dip

Strawberry Fruit Dip

Marsha Dixon
Bella Vista, AR

This recipe is always a smash hit at the annual ladies' luncheon that I have with the women of my church...a Mothers' Day must-have.

8-oz. pkg. strawberry-flavored
    cream cheese, softened
2 T. strawberry preserves
7-oz. jar marshmallow creme

8-oz. container frozen whipped
    topping, thawed
assorted sliced fresh fruit

Beat together cream cheese and preserves until well blended. Fold in marshmallow creme and whipped topping. Cover and refrigerate until serving. Serve with fruit. Makes 4 cups.

Pineapple Wassail

Jennie Gist
Gooseberry Patch

Perfect for a holiday open house or church social.

4 c. unsweetened pineapple juice
12-oz. can apricot nectar
2 c. apple cider
1-1/2 c. orange juice

2 4-inch cinnamon sticks
1 t. whole cloves
4 cardamom seeds, crushed

Combine all ingredients in a saucepan; bring to a boil over high heat. Reduce heat to low and and simmer 15 to 20 minutes. To serve, strain into serving glasses or a punch bowl. Serve warm. Makes about 2 quarts.

Baked Brie with Figs

Marian Buckley
Fontana, CA

My adult Sunday school class had all agreed to bring dishes for an Old Testament foods potluck. I was really stumped for something to take until I found this recipe. Figs...perfect! And it's delicious.

2 T. water
1/2 c. brown sugar, packed
6 fresh figs or 10 dried figs,
   chopped

1 t. vanilla extract, divided
1/2 c. toasted slivered almonds
14-oz. pkg. Brie cheese round
round buttery crackers

Combine water and brown sugar in a small saucepan. Cook over medium heat, stirring often, until brown sugar is completely dissolved. Add figs and 1/2 teaspoon vanilla. Simmer until figs are softened, about 10 minutes. Stir in remaining vanilla and almonds. Place cheese round in an ungreased one-quart round casserole dish. Spoon fig mixture over the top. Bake, uncovered, at 325 degrees for 10 to 15 minutes, until softened but not melted. Serve warm with crackers. Makes 10 servings.

For an easy yet elegant appetizer, try a cheese platter. Choose a soft cheese, a hard cheese and a semi-soft or crumbly cheese. Add a basket of crisp crackers, crusty baguette slices and some sliced apples or pears. So simple, yet sure to please everyone!

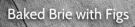
Baked Brie with Figs

Spinach Party Puffs

Spinach Party Puffs

Vickie
Gooseberry Patch

We love these flavorful bite-size morsels! The unbaked puffs can even be frozen...no need to thaw before baking. Terrific for last-minute celebrations!

10-oz. pkg. frozen chopped
  spinach
1/2 c. onion, chopped
2 eggs, lightly beaten
1/2 c. grated Parmesan cheese
1/2 c. shredded Cheddar cheese

1/2 c. blue cheese salad dressing
1/4 c. butter, melted and slightly
  cooled
1/8 t. garlic powder
8-1/2 oz. pkg. cornbread mix

In a saucepan, cook spinach according to package directions, adding onion at the same time. Drain spinach well and press out any excess liquid; set aside. In a large bowl, combine remaining ingredients except cornbread mix. Add spinach mixture and dry cornbread mix; stir well. Cover and chill until firm; form dough into one-inch balls. Cover and chill until serving time. Place chilled puffs on an ungreased baking sheet. Bake at 350 degrees for 10 to 12 minutes, until lightly golden. Makes about 5 dozen.

197

Curry Chicken Party Rolls

Paulette Walters
Newfoundland, Canada

I love being able to make this tasty appetizer with ingredients I already have on hand. It makes a lot of servings and takes no time at all! You can even use raisins or apples instead of grapes.

1 boneless, skinless chicken breast,
  cooked and shredded
3 to 4 T. mayonnaise
2 to 3 T. grapes, thinly sliced

2 T. celery, finely diced
curry powder to taste
3 soft sandwich wraps

In a bowl, mix chicken with just enough mayonnaise to hold together. Add grapes, celery and curry powder. Spread mixture on wraps and roll up; cut into one-inch lengths. Serve immediately, or cover and refrigerate until serving time. Makes 8 to 10 servings.

Pecan-Stuffed Deviled Eggs

Jo Ann
Gooseberry Patch

Top with additional parsley and chopped pecans for a festive presentation.

6 eggs, hard-boiled and peeled
1/4 c. mayonnaise
1 t. onion, grated
1/2 t. fresh parsley, chopped

1/2 t. dry mustard
1/8 t. salt
1/3 c. pecans, coarsely chopped
Garnish: fresh parsley

Cut eggs in half lengthwise and carefully remove yolks. Mash yolks in a small bowl. Add mayonnaise, onion, parsley, mustard and salt; blend well. Stir in pecans. Spoon or pipe yolk mixture evenly into egg-white halves. Makes one dozen.

198

If you're going to make hard-boiled eggs, use eggs that have been refrigerated at least 7 to 10 days, instead of fresher eggs...the shells will slip right off.

Pecan-Stuffed Deviled Eggs

Antipasto

Antipasto

Doreen DeRosa
New Castle, PA

This recipe will feed a crowd! Keep it handy when you need something that's easy and can be made ahead. Serve with a slotted spoon or provide toothpicks for your guests.

1 lb. Cheddar cheese, cubed
1 lb. provolone cheese, cubed
1 lb. sliced mushrooms
1 lb. hard salami, cubed
1/2 lb. pepperoni, cubed
6-oz. can whole pitted ripe black
   olives, drained

1 onion, chopped
1 green pepper, chopped
1 jalapeño pepper, sliced
16-oz. bottle Italian salad dressing

Toss together all ingredients in a serving bowl. Cover and chill overnight. Makes 18 cups.

For large celebrations, try hosting an afternoon open house instead of a sit-down dinner. A buffet of light finger foods and beverages is fun for drop-in guests and easy on the budget.

White Chicken Pizza

*Michelle Schuberg
Big Rapids, MI*

A quick & easy dinner even your most finicky eaters will love!

13.8-oz. can refrigerated pizza
   crust dough
1 T. olive oil
2 boneless, skinless chicken
   breasts, cubed
2 T. garlic, minced

15-oz. jar Alfredo pasta sauce
1/2 c. onion, chopped
8-oz. pkg. shredded mozzarella,
   Parmesan & Romano-blend
   cheese

Spread dough onto a lightly greased pizza baking pan; bake at 425 degrees
for 7 minutes. Meanwhile, heat oil in a skillet over medium heat. Sauté
chicken and garlic until chicken juices run clear when pierced. Spread
Alfredo sauce over baked crust; sprinkle with chicken and onion. Bake
at 425 degrees for 10 minutes; top with cheese and return to oven for
5 minutes, or until cheese melts. Serves 8.

Scrumptious Olive Bread

*Kym Cicero
Bristow, VA*

*The men in the family ask for this all the time! A favorite at potluck
suppers and parties, this bread is great as an hors d'oeuvre and
deliciously complements any pasta dish. It freezes well and reheats
easily in the microwave.*

1 to 1-1/2 4-oz. jars green olives,
   drained and well minced
1/2 c. mayonnaise
1/2 c. butter, melted

8-oz. pkg. shredded Monterey Jack
   cheese
1 large wide loaf French bread,
   sliced in half lengthwise

Mix olives, mayonnaise, butter and cheese in a large bowl, blending well.
Spread mixture over cut sides of bread; place on a baking sheet. Bake,
uncovered, at 350 degrees for 15 minutes, or until golden and cheese is
melted. Slice and serve warm. Makes about 16 servings.

White Chicken Pizza

Michelle's Caramel Corn

Michelle's Caramel Corn

Michelle Sheridan
Athens, AL

Oh-so light, sweet and crunchy...yum!

12 c. popped popcorn
1 c. dark brown sugar, packed
1/2 c. light corn syrup
1/3 c. butter
1 T. light molasses
1-1/2 t. vanilla extract
1/2 t. baking soda
1/2 t. salt

Spray a large roaster pan with non-stick vegetable spray. Place popcorn in pan and set aside. In a saucepan over medium heat, combine brown sugar, corn syrup, butter and molasses. Bring to a boil; cook for 5 minutes, stirring once. Remove from heat; stir in vanilla, baking soda and salt. Pour hot mixture over popcorn, stirring to coat. Bake at 250 degrees for one hour, stirring every 15 minutes. Remove from oven; stir to break up. Cool for 15 minutes. Store in an airtight container for up to one week. Makes about 12 cups.

Set up old-timey games like badminton and croquet for an icebreaker that will bring all ages together! Indoors, try favorite board games or even a big jigsaw puzzle.

White Chocolate Party Mix

Lecia Stevenson
Timberville, VA

My sister Lena is always making the most delicious snacks! I ask for the recipes and they are always fast and easy. She gave me this party mix one year for a Christmas gift. I totally enjoyed it and now I make it myself.

5 c. doughnut-shaped oat cereal
5 c. bite-size crispy corn cereal squares
10-oz. pkg. mini pretzel twists
2 c. salted peanuts
16-oz. pkg. candy-coated chocolates
2 12-oz. pkgs. white chocolate chips
3 T. oil

In a large heat-proof bowl, combine cereals, pretzels, peanuts and candy-coated chocolates. Toss to mix; set aside. Combine white chocolate chips and oil in a microwave-safe bowl. Microwave on medium-high for 2 minutes, stirring once. Continue to microwave on high at 30-second intervals; stir until smooth. Pour chocolate mixture over cereal mixture and stir well to coat. Spread onto 3 wax paper-lined baking sheets to cool completely. Break apart when cool. Store in an airtight container. Makes 20 cups.

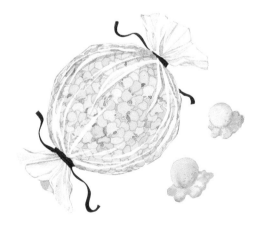

For fun party favors, fill clear plastic cups with crunchy snack mix. Seal with sheets of colorful plastic wrap to keep the goodies inside. Heap the cups in a basket...guests can choose a favorite to take home.

White Chocolate Party Mix

Roasted Red Pepper Spread

Roasted Red Pepper Spread

Donna Cannon
Tulsa, OK

For years, my large Italian family would come together at one of our homes for Christmas Eve or post-Christmas get-togethers. We each signed up to bring appetizers, main dishes, side dishes, desserts and beverages. This delicious spread was always a favorite.

8-oz. container mayonnaise
8-oz. container sour cream
7-oz. jar roasted red peppers, drained and liquid reserved
1 handful fresh basil, loosely packed
salt and pepper to taste
Melba toast rounds, snack crackers, vegetable slices

In a food processor, combine mayonnaise and sour cream. Add peppers, basil, salt and pepper; pulse until well-combined. Blend in reserved liquid, one tablespoon at a time, to desired consistency. Spoon into a serving dish or bread bowl. Serve with Melba toast, crackers or vegetables. Makes 2 to 3 cups.

209

Sweet & Simple Lemonade

Zoe Bennett
Columbia, SC

As easy as 1-2-3...there's nothing like real lemonade!

2 c. lemon juice
1 c. superfine sugar
8 c. water
ice cubes

Combine lemon juice and sugar in a pitcher; stir until sugar is dissolved. Add cold water, mixing well. Cover and chill; serve over ice. Makes 10 servings.

Festive Cranberry-Cheese Spread

Arlene Smulski
Lyons, IL

This cheery appetizer is perfect for parties during the holiday season. It has a very short prep time and both adults and kids will gobble it up.

8-oz. pkg. cream cheese, softened
1/2 c. sweetened dried cranberries, chopped
1/2 c. dried apricots, chopped
1/4 c. chopped walnuts
1 t. orange zest
assorted crackers or party rye bread

In a large bowl, combine all ingredients except crackers or bread. Beat until well blended. Cover and chill until serving time. Serve with crackers or party rye slices. Serves 8 to 10.

210

Serve up a favorite creamy dip in bite-size cucumber cups. Slice cukes into chunks and scoop out the centers with a melon baller. Fill them with dip and set on a platter, garnished with fresh herb sprigs if you like.

Festive Cranberry-Cheese Spread

Festive trimmings can turn the simplest fare into a feast. Pick up some brightly colored napkins and table coverings at the nearest dollar store and you're halfway to a party!

 Fill out a buffet frugally with bite-size comfort foods that everyone loves. Meatballs in sauce, deviled eggs, marinated olives and garlic bread are just a few ideas for inexpensive, easy-to-make party treats.

 To keep party beverages from watering down, freeze iced tea or lemonade in ice cube trays and use in place of ordinary ice.

At your next get-together, set out a guest book! Ask everyone young and old to sign...it will become a treasured journal of the occasion.

Heavenly
Desserts

Cocoa & Coffee Sheet Cake

Patricia Ivey
Lamar, AR

My family really enjoys this scrumptious cake! Perfect for an after-church fellowship hour.

2 c. all-purpose flour
2 c. sugar
1/2 c. shortening
1/4 c. baking cocoa
1 c. brewed coffee
1/2 c. butter

1 t. baking soda
1 t. vanilla extract
1/2 c. buttermilk
1 t. cinnamon
2 eggs, beaten

Combine flour and sugar in a large bowl; set aside. In a saucepan, combine shortening, cocoa, coffee and butter; bring to a boil. Slowly stir into flour mixture. Batter will resemble fudge. Stir in baking soda, vanilla, buttermilk, cinnamon and eggs, mixing until well blended. Pour batter into a greased and floured 13"x9" baking pan. Bake at 400 degrees for 25 minutes. Remove cake from oven; immediately pour Frosting over cake. Makes 24 servings.

Frosting:

1/4 c. baking cocoa
6 T. milk
1/2 c. butter

16-oz. pkg. powdered sugar
1 t. vanilla extract
1/2 c. chopped pecans

In a large saucepan over medium heat, combine cocoa, milk and butter; bring to a boil. Add powdered sugar, vanilla and pecans, stirring well.

Set up an ice cream buffet! Offer 2 or 3 flavors of ice cream, sweet toppings and a plate of cookies for nibbling. Easy for you, fun for guests!

Cocoa & Coffee Sheet Cake

German Apple Streusel Kuchen

German Apple Streusel Kuchen

Karin Anderson
Hillsboro, OH

I was born and raised in Germany, so naturally I am always looking for recipes reminding me of my German childhood. Baking this cake brings back so many beautiful memories of my parents and brothers.

16-oz. loaf frozen bread dough, thawed
4 Granny Smith apples, peeled, cored and thinly sliced
3/4 c. plus 1/3 c. sugar, divided
1 t. cinnamon
1 T. vanilla extract
1/4 c. sliced almonds
1-1/4 c. all-purpose flour
1/4 c. butter, melted

Let dough rise according to package directions. Spread dough on a greased 16"x11" jelly-roll pan. Cover dough with plastic wrap sprayed with non-stick spray. Let rise in a warm place (85 degrees), free from drafts, 20 to 25 minutes, until double in size. Combine apples, 3/4 cup sugar, cinnamon and vanilla; spread apple mixture evenly over dough. Sprinkle with almonds. Combine flour, butter and remaining sugar in a separate bowl; mix until crumbly and spread evenly over apple layer. Bake at 375 degrees for 25 minutes, or until a toothpick inserted in the center comes out clean. Cool completely in pan on a wire rack; cut into squares. Makes 2 dozen.

Brown Sugar Cake

Cindy Lyzenga
Zeeland, MI

This cake is easy and fun to make! It is always a hit at our church potlucks and I never take home any leftovers.

18-1/2 oz. pkg. white cake mix
3.4-oz. pkg. instant vanilla pudding mix
2 eggs, beaten
2 c. milk
3/4 c. brown sugar, packed
3/4 c. semi-sweet chocolate chips

In a large bowl, stir together dry cake and pudding mixes, eggs and milk. Pour batter into a greased 13"x9" baking pan. Sprinkle brown sugar and chocolate chips over batter. Bake at 375 degrees for 30 to 35 minutes, until cake tests done with a toothpick. Makes 12 servings.

Brenda's Fruit Crisp

Brenda Smith
Delaware, OH

Here's my favorite dessert recipe...it's a yummy way to use a bumper crop of peaches, apples or berries!

5 c. frozen peaches, apples or berries, thawed and juices reserved
2 to 4 T. sugar
1/2 c. long-cooking oats, uncooked
1/2 c. brown sugar, packed
1/4 c. all-purpose flour
1/4 t. vanilla extract
1/4 t. nutmeg
1/4 t. cinnamon
Optional: 1/4 c. sweetened flaked coconut
1/4 c. butter, diced
Garnish: vanilla ice cream

Place fruit and reserved juices in an ungreased 2-quart casserole dish; stir in sugar and set aside. Mix oats, brown sugar, flour, vanilla and spices in a bowl. Stir in coconut, if using. Add butter to oat mixture; mix with a fork until mixture is the texture of coarse crumbs. Sprinkle over fruit. Bake at 375 degrees for 30 to 35 minutes, until topping is golden and fruit is tender. Serve warm, topped with a scoop of ice cream. Serves 6.

For a super-easy summertime treat, fill an enamelware pail with crushed ice and lots of fresh fruit. Picnic perfect because it's easy to tote and the fruit stays nice and chilled.

Brenda's Fruit Crisp

Angel Strudel

Angel Strudel

Jo Baker
Litchfield, IL

This is one of my favorite recipes from my grandmother's farm home, where we kept busy from morning until night.

1 c. butter
2 c. all-purpose flour
3 egg yolks
2 T. vinegar
1/4 c. water

1 c. walnuts, ground
1 c. maraschino cherries, chopped
18-1/4 oz. pkg. angel food cake
    mix

In a large bowl, cut butter into flour until mixture resembles coarse crumbs; set aside. In a separate bowl, whisk together egg yolks, vinegar and water; add to butter mixture and stir well. Divide dough into 4 portions; cover and refrigerate for 8 hours to overnight. When ready to prepare strudel, roll out one portion of dough on a floured surface into a very thin rectangle. In a bowl, combine walnuts, cherries and dry cake mix; divide into 4 equal portions. Spread one portion of walnut filling on one dough rectangle. Roll up, starting at one short edge. Repeat with remaining 3 portions of filling and dough. Place each on an ungreased baking sheet. Bake each strudel at 325 degrees for 25 minutes. Slice to serve. Makes 4 strudels; each serves 8 to 10.

221

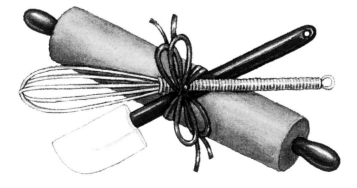

'Tis the sweet, simple things of life which are the real ones after all.
-Laura Ingalls Wilder

Caramel-Glazed Apple Cake

Brenda Smith
Delaware, OH

This made-from-scratch cake with its luscious glaze is irresistible! It's also easy to carry to get-togethers or potlucks right in its baking pan.

1-1/2 c. butter, softened
1 c. sugar
1 c. brown sugar, packed
3 eggs
3 c. all-purpose flour
1 t. baking soda
1/2 t. salt

2 t. cinnamon
1/2 t. nutmeg
5 Granny Smith apples, peeled, cored and diced
1-1/4 c. chopped pecans
2-1/4 t. vanilla extract

In a large bowl, combine butter and sugars. Beat with an electric mixer on medium-high speed until light and fluffy. Beat in eggs, one at a time; set aside. In a separate bowl, combine flour, baking soda, salt and spices. Using a wooden spoon, gradually add flour mixture to butter mixture to form a very thick batter. Stir in remaining ingredients. Pour batter into a greased and floured 13"x9" baking pan. Bake at 325 degrees for 50 to 60 minutes, until a toothpick inserted in the center comes out clean. Cool cake in pan on a wire rack for at least 10 minutes. Poke holes all over surface of cake with a fork. Pour warm Caramel Glaze over cake. Serve warm or cooled. Serves 16.

Caramel Glaze:

1/4 c. butter
1/4 c. sugar
1/4 c. brown sugar, packed

1/8 t. salt
1/2 c. whipping cream

Melt butter in a saucepan over medium-low heat. Add sugars and salt. Cook, stirring often, for 2 minutes. Stir in cream and bring to a boil. Cook, stirring constantly, for 2 minutes.

Here's a slick trick for cutting a cake with sticky frosting! Between slices, simply dip the knife in hot water and wipe it clean with a paper towel.

Caramel-Glazed Apple Cake

Oh-So-Easy Peach Cobbler

Oh-So-Easy Peach Cobbler

Dueley Lucas
Somerset, KY

Wonderful topped with vanilla ice cream or a splash of milk...
or even all by itself!

2 15-oz. cans sliced peaches,
   drained and 1/2 c. juice reserved
1/2 c. butter, sliced
1 c. self-rising flour
1 c. sugar
1 c. milk

Arrange peaches in a 13"x9" baking pan that has been sprayed with non-stick vegetable spray. Pour in reserved juice. Arrange butter slices over peaches; set aside. In a bowl, mix flour, sugar and milk, stirring until smooth. Spoon batter over peaches, spreading to the edges of pan. Bake at 375 degrees for 30 minutes, or until golden. Serve warm. Serves 10 to 12.

Southern Iced Tea

Anna Brown
Tahlequah, OK

I like to use decaffeinated tea...I think it tastes smoother.

4 family-size tea bags
1-1/2 c. water
1-1/2 c. sugar
ice cubes
Garnish: lemon or orange slices,
   fresh mint sprigs

Combine tea bags and water in a microwave-safe 2-cup glass container. Microwave on high setting for 4 to 5 minutes. Add sugar to a heatproof one-gallon pitcher. Pour hot tea over sugar; gently squeeze excess tea from tea bags. Stir well until sugar is dissolved; add enough cold water to fill pitcher. Serve over ice; garnish as desired. Makes one gallon.

Crustless Pumpkin Pie

Linda Webb
Delaware, OH

My favorite pumpkin dessert...too good to save only for Thanksgiving!

4 eggs, beaten
15-oz. can pumpkin
12-oz. can evaporated milk
1-1/2 c. sugar
2 t. pumpkin pie spice
1 t. salt

18-1/2 oz. pkg. yellow cake mix
1 c. chopped pecans or walnuts
1 c. butter, melted
Garnish: whipped topping, chopped
  nuts, cinnamon

In a large bowl, combine eggs, pumpkin, evaporated milk, sugar, spice and salt. Mix well; pour into an ungreased 13"x9" baking pan. Sprinkle dry cake mix and nuts over top. Drizzle with melted butter; do not stir. Bake at 350 degrees for 45 minutes to one hour, testing for doneness with a toothpick. Serve garnished with a dollop of whipped topping, sprinkled with nuts and cinnamon. Makes 8 to 10 servings.

226

For a new twist, spoon pie servings into pretty parfait cups and top with dollops of whipped cream.

Crustless Pumpkin Pie

Cheesecake Cranberry Bars

Cheesecake Cranberry Bars

Linda Galvin
Ames, IA

Baking for a holiday party or bake sale? These pebbly-topped bars will disappear in a flash.

2 c. all-purpose flour
1-1/2 c. long-cooking oats, uncooked
1/4 c. brown sugar, packed
1 c. butter, softened
12-oz. pkg. white chocolate chips
8-oz. pkg. cream cheese, softened
14-oz. can sweetened condensed milk
1/4 c. lemon juice
1 t. vanilla extract
14-oz. can whole-berry cranberry sauce
2 T. cornstarch

In a large bowl, combine flour, oats and brown sugar; cut in butter until coarse crumbs form. Stir in chocolate chips; set aside 2-1/2 cups of crumb mixture for topping. With floured fingers, press remaining crumb mixture into a greased 13"x9" baking pan; set aside. Beat cream cheese in a large bowl until creamy. Add condensed milk, lemon juice and vanilla; stir until smooth. Pour cream cheese mixture over crust. Combine cranberry sauce and cornstarch; spoon over cream cheese mixture. Sprinkle reserved crumb mixture over top. Bake at 375 degrees for 35 to 40 minutes, or until golden. Let cool and cut into bars. Makes 2 dozen.

If you see a vintage cake pan with its own slide-on lid at a tag sale, snap it up! It's indispensable for toting cakes and bar cookies to church socials and picnics.

Tennessee Fudge Pie

Dusty Cannon
Paxton, IL

Mama has always made this pie for our Thanksgiving. People request it for church socials and parties too...it's a chocolate lover's dream!

2 eggs
1/2 c. butter, melted and cooled
   slightly
1/4 c. baking cocoa
1/4 c. all-purpose flour
1 c. sugar

2 t. vanilla extract
1/3 c. semi-sweet chocolate chips
1/3 c. chopped pecans
9-inch pie crust, unbaked
Garnish: whipped cream, chocolate
   curls

In a bowl, beat eggs slightly; stir in melted butter. Add remaining ingredients except crust and garnish; mix well and pour into unbaked crust. Bake at 350 degrees for about 25 minutes, until firm. Cool completely before slicing; garnish as desired. Makes 8 servings.

Minister's Delight

Marsha Baker
Pioneer, OH

My youth pastor's wife gave me this recipe. It's a scrumptious Sunday dessert that can be left to cook in the slow cooker while you're away at church. Very simple and versatile...oh-so delicious!

21-oz. can apple, cherry, blueberry
   or peach pie filling
Optional: 1 c. crushed pineapple,
   partially drained
18-oz. pkg. yellow cake mix

1/2 c. butter, melted
Optional: 1/3 c. chopped walnuts or
   pecans
Garnish: ice cream or whipped
   topping

Spray a slow cooker with non-stick vegetable spray. Add pie filling; spread pineapple over top, if using. In a bowl, combine dry cake mix and butter; mix with a fork until crumbly. Sprinkle over pie filling. Sprinkle nuts on top, if desired. Place 2 paper towels on top of slow cooker to catch any condensation. Cover and cook on low setting for 2 to 3 hours. Serve warm with ice cream or whipped topping. Makes 5 to 6 servings.

Tennessee Fudge Pie

County Fair Grand Champion Cake

County Fair Grand Champion Cake

Cindy Conway
Elizabeth, CO

You'll never believe the surprise ingredient that makes this cake a winner...it's beets!

2 c. all-purpose flour
2 t. baking soda
1/4 t. salt
3 1-oz. sqs. semi-sweet baking
  chocolate
1 c. oil, divided
2 15-oz. cans sliced beets, drained
1-3/4 c. sugar
3 eggs, beaten
1 t. vanilla extract
Garnish: baking cocoa, powdered
  sugar

Mix together flour, baking soda and salt; set aside. Melt chocolate with 1/4 cup oil in a double boiler; stir until smooth and set aside. Purée beets in a blender; measure 2 cups and set aside. Blend sugar and eggs in a large bowl; gradually mix in remaining oil, pureéd beets, melted chocolate and vanilla. Stir in flour mixture; mix well. Grease a Bundt® pan and dust with cocoa; pour batter into pan. Bake at 375 degrees for one hour, or until a toothpick tests clean. Cool for 15 minutes on a wire rack. Turn out cake; dust with powdered sugar. Makes 10 to 12 servings.

233

Better Than Brownies

Gladys Kielar
Whitehouse, OH

If you love brownies, you'll like these baked goodies even better! These are so easy and always come out right. They are a favorite at our teacher staff meetings.

3.4-oz. pkg. cook & serve chocolate
  pudding mix
2 c. milk
18-1/2 oz. pkg. chocolate cake mix
1 c. semi-sweet chocolate chips
1 c. chopped nuts

Prepare dry pudding mix with milk according to package directions; cook until slightly thickened. Remove from heat. Stir in dry cake mix. Spread batter in a greased 13"x9" baking pan; sprinkle with chocolate chips and nuts. Bake at 350 degrees for 30 minutes. Cool; cut into squares. Makes about 2 dozen.

Peanut Butter Texas Sheet Cake

Kathi Rostash
Nevada, OH

Attention, peanut butter lovers! This moist cake has peanut butter baked inside the cake and mixed into the icing...plus a sprinkling of peanuts on top!

2 c. all-purpose flour	1/4 c. creamy peanut butter
2 c. sugar	2 eggs, beaten
1/2 t. salt	1 t. vanilla extract
1 t. baking soda	1/2 c. buttermilk
1 c. butter	Garnish: chopped peanuts
1 c. water	

Combine flour, sugar, salt and baking soda in a large bowl; set aside. Combine butter, water and peanut butter in a saucepan over medium heat; bring to a boil. Add to flour mixture and mix well; set aside. Combine eggs, vanilla and buttermilk; add to peanut butter mixture. Spread batter in a greased 15"x10" jelly-roll pan. Bake at 350 degrees for 25 to 28 minutes, until cake springs back when gently touched. Spread Peanut Butter Icing over warm cake; sprinkle with peanuts. Serves 15 to 20.

Peanut Butter Icing:

1/2 c. butter	16-oz. pkg. powdered sugar
1/4 c. creamy peanut butter	1 t. vanilla extract
1/3 c. plus 1 T. milk	

Combine butter, peanut butter and milk in a large saucepan over medium heat; bring to a boil. Remove from heat. Stir in powdered sugar and vanilla; stir to a spreading consistency.

Keep plastic wrap from sticking to a frosted cake. Stick mini marshmallows on the ends of toothpicks, then insert into the cake. Gently cover with plastic wrap...the toothpicks won't poke holes through the wrap!

Peanut Butter Texas Sheet Cake

Chocolate Zucchini Cupcakes

Chocolate Zucchini Cupcakes

Michelle Sheridan
Athens, AL

So moist and delicious...no one will guess the secret ingredient is zucchini!

2 c. zucchini, shredded
3 eggs, beaten
2 c. sugar
3/4 c. oil
2 t. vanilla extract
2 c. all-purpose flour

2/3 c. baking cocoa
1/2 t. baking powder
1 t. baking soda
1 t. salt
3/4 c. milk chocolate chips

Combine zucchini, eggs, sugar, oil and vanilla in a large bowl; mix well. Add flour, cocoa, baking powder, baking soda and salt; stir well. Fold in chocolate chips. Spoon batter into paper-lined muffin cups, filling 2/3 full. Bake at 325 degrees for 25 minutes, or until a toothpick inserted near center tests clean. Cool in muffin tin for 5 minutes. Remove cupcakes from tin; cool completely. Frost with Peanut Butter Frosting. Makes 2 dozen.

237

Peanut Butter Frosting:

1/2 c. creamy peanut butter
1/3 c. butter, softened
1 T. milk

1/2 t. vanilla extract
1-1/2 c. powdered sugar

Beat peanut butter, butter, milk and vanilla until smooth. Gradually beat in powdered sugar.

Put a tiered pie stand to work serving up cookies, cupcakes and other goodies. It takes up less room on a buffet table and looks so special.

Hokey-Pokey Cupcakes

Veva Banks
Neosho, MO

These scrumptious cupcakes have a surprise swirl of fruit flavor inside. You can easily swap different flavors of gelatin and frosting to match the occasion.

18-1/4 oz. pkg. white cake mix
3-oz. pkg. orange gelatin mix
1 c. boiling water

16-oz. container favorite-flavor frosting

Prepare cake mix according to package directions, using egg white version. Spoon batter into 24 paper-lined muffin cups; bake as directed. Let cupcakes cool in muffin tin for 15 minutes. Spray a large fork with non-stick vegetable spray; pierce cupcakes with fork at 1/4-inch intervals. Place cupcakes on a paper towel-lined tray; set aside. Add gelatin mix to boiling water, stirring until dissolved; spoon over cupcakes. Chill cupcakes for 3 hours. Frost and garnish as desired. Makes 2 dozen.

Heavenly Drop Cookies

Cathy Hinkley
Colon, MI

Twenty years ago, while I was working at a grocery store over the holidays, a store patron gave me this cookie recipe. It's still a favorite with my family for all holidays! I'll use colored or white sugar to match the different holidays...so pretty on a cookie tray.

2 c. margarine
16-oz. pkg. powdered sugar
3 eggs, beaten
1 T. hot water

1 T. vanilla extract
5 c. all-purpose flour
2 t. baking soda
Garnish: colored sugar

Blend together margarine and powdered sugar in a very large bowl. Add eggs, water and vanilla; stir until fluffy. Gradually add flour and baking soda; mix well. Cover and chill for 30 minutes. Drop dough by teaspoonfuls into a bowl of colored sugar; lightly roll around to coat. Place on greased baking sheets. Bake at 350 degrees for 10 to 12 minutes. Makes about 6 dozen.

Blueberry Pound Cake

Blueberry Pound Cake

Suzy Grubich
Eighty Four, PA

I entered this cake in the county fair and won second place. A chocolate cake beat it out for the blue ribbon...it's tough to beat chocolate!

2-1/2 c. sugar
1/2 c. butter, softened
2 t. vanilla extract
8-oz. pkg. cream cheese, softened
4 eggs
2 c. fresh blueberries

3 c. all-purpose flour, divided
1 t. baking powder
1/2 t. baking soda
1/2 t. salt
8-oz. container lemon yogurt

Combine sugar, butter, vanilla and cream cheese in a large bowl. Beat with an electric mixer on medium speed until blended. Beat in eggs, one at a time. Toss blueberries with 2 tablespoons flour; set aside. Combine remaining flour, baking powder, baking soda and salt. Add flour mixture to sugar mixture alternately with yogurt; beat well. Fold in blueberries; pour into a greased tube pan. Bake at 350 degrees for one hour, or until a toothpick tests done. Cool cake in pan for 10 minutes; turn out onto a cake plate. Drizzle with Powdered Sugar Icing while still warm. Serves 16.

241

Powdered Sugar Icing:

1/2 c. powdered sugar   4 t. lemon juice

Combine ingredients to a drizzling consistency.

An old-fashioned cake or pie auction makes a great fundraiser.
Tuck each treat in a decorated box and let the bidding begin!

Red Velvet Cake

Peggy Frazier
Indianapolis, IN

When my daughter Julie was young, I helped her make this cake for a fundraiser. She won first prize and still has the blue ribbon!

2-1/2 c. all-purpose flour	2 eggs, beaten
1-1/2 c. sugar	1 t. vanilla extract
1 t. salt	1-oz. bottle red food coloring
1 t. baking cocoa	1 t. white vinegar
1 c. buttermilk	1 t. baking soda
1-1/2 c. oil	

In a large bowl, mix flour, sugar, salt and cocoa. Add buttermilk, oil, eggs and vanilla; beat well. Stir in food coloring. Mix vinegar and baking soda; add to batter and stir just until well blended. Pour batter into 3 greased and floured 9" round cake pans. Bake at 325 degrees for 30 to 35 minutes, until a toothpick tests done. Cool; turn out layers and assemble with Cream Cheese Frosting. Serves 10 to 12.

Cream Cheese Frosting:

8-oz. pkg. cream cheese, softened	6 c. powdered sugar
1/2 c. butter, softened	Optional: chopped pecans
1 t. vanilla extract	

Beat cream cheese, butter and vanilla until blended. Stir in powdered sugar until smooth; add nuts, if using.

Before frosting layered cakes, wrap individual layers in plastic wrap and freeze overnight. Remove and frost right away...it's so easy to spread frosting and the cake stays moist longer!

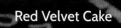
Red Velvet Cake

Frosted Banana Bars

Frosted Banana Bars

Karen Sampson
Waymart, PA

This is a recipe that's great for church bake sales. It's also wonderful for our social time after church when we get to enjoy refreshments and fellowship. Best of all, it's quick, easy, moist and delicious!

1/2 c. butter, softened	1 t. vanilla extract
2 c. sugar	2 c. all-purpose flour
3 eggs, beaten	1 t. baking soda
1-1/2 c. ripe bananas, mashed	1/2 t. salt
1/4 c. applesauce	Optional: chopped nuts

Beat together butter and sugar in a large bowl. Beat in eggs, bananas, applesauce and vanilla; set aside. In a separate bowl, combine flour, baking soda and salt; add to butter mixture, mixing well. Spread in a greased 15"x10" jelly-roll pan. Bake at 350 degrees for 25 minutes, or until bars test done. Cool completely; spread with Frosting. Garnish with nuts, if desired. Makes 3 dozen.

Frosting:

1/2 c. butter, softened	16-oz. pkg. powdered sugar
8-oz. pkg. cream cheese, softened	2 t. vanilla extract

Beat butter and cream cheese together in a large bowl. Gradually add powdered sugar and vanilla; beat well.

A plate of cookies is a sweet way to say "Thanks!" to a youth leader... it shows how much you appreciate her talents and time.

Velvety Lime Squares

Kathy Unruh
Fresno, CA

*A variety of ingredients come together to make this spectacular dessert.
I think you'll agree...it's a hit!*

3-oz. can sweetened flaked
  coconut, divided
2 c. vanilla wafer crumbs
2 T. butter, melted
2 T. sugar
2 3-oz. pkgs. lime gelatin mix
2 c. boiling water

6-oz. can frozen limeade
  concentrate
3 pts. vanilla ice cream, softened
1/8 t. salt
3 drops green food coloring
Optional: slivered almonds

Spread 1/2 cup coconut on a baking sheet. Toast at 375 degrees until lightly golden, about 5 minutes; set aside. Combine remaining coconut, vanilla wafer crumbs, melted butter and sugar in a bowl; press into an ungreased 11"x7" baking pan. Bake at 375 degrees for 6 to 7 minutes; cool. Dissolve gelatin in boiling water; add limeade, ice cream, salt and food coloring, stirring until smooth. Spread gelatin mixture in baked crust; sprinkle with toasted coconut and almonds, if desired. Cover tightly; freeze until firm. To serve, let stand at room temperature 20 minutes; cut into squares to serve. Serves 15.

Lemon Fluff

Janice Reinhardt
Bethel Park, PA

*This dessert was especially enjoyed by my dad. I would bake it
for his birthday celebrations.*

18-1/4 oz. pkg. lemon cake mix
8-oz. pkg. cream cheese, softened
3-oz. pkg. cream cheese, softened
3 c. milk

2 3.4-oz. pkgs. instant lemon
  pudding mix
12-oz. container frozen whipped
  topping, thawed

Prepare cake mix according to package instructions; bake in a greased and floured 13"x9" baking pan. Let cool. In a large bowl, beat cream cheese with an electric mixer on medium speed until smooth. Add milk and pudding mixes; beat for 5 minutes, then spread over cooled cake. Top with whipped topping. Cover and refrigerate; serve chilled. Serves 12 to 15.

Velvety Lime Squares

Grandma & Katie's Frozen Dessert

Heavenly Desserts

Grandma & Katie's Frozen Dessert

Jennifer Brown
Garden Grove, CA

Refreshing during the summer, or any time of year! This tasty no-bake treat can be made ahead of time. It's a big hit with kids and makes enough to feed the whole Sunday School class.

1/2 c. creamy peanut butter
1/2 c. light corn syrup
2 c. crispy rice cereal
2 c. chocolate-flavored crispy rice cereal

1/2 gal. vanilla ice cream, softened
1/2 to 1 c. Spanish peanuts, coarsely chopped
Optional: chocolate syrup

Blend together peanut butter and corn syrup in a large bowl. Add cereals; stir until coated. Press into the bottom of an ungreased 13"x9" baking pan. Spread ice cream over cereal mixture; sprinkle with peanuts. Swirl chocolate syrup over top, if desired. Cover with aluminum foil; freeze at least 4 hours before serving. Cut into squares to serve. Serves 15 to 18.

Golden Punch

Shannon Reents
Loudonville, OH

I like to use autumn colors in everything, even food and beverages! This yummy punch is easy to change for the holiday. Just use orange gelatin mix for Halloween, red strawberry for Christmas and so forth. Enjoy!

6-oz. pkg. lemon gelatin mix
3/4 c. sugar
2 c. hot water
46-oz. can unsweetened pineapple juice

12-oz. can frozen lemonade concentrate, thawed
4 ltrs. lemon-lime soda, chilled

In a large bowl, dissolve gelatin mix and sugar in hot water. Add pineapple juice and lemonade. Mix well; pour into a freezer container. Cover and freeze. Shortly before serving time, remove from freezer; add to a punch bowl and let thaw slightly. Add desired amount of chilled soda; stir gently. Makes 15 to 20 servings.

Strawberry Pizza

Micki Stephens
Marion, OH

With a sugar cookie crust, a cream cheese "sauce" and fresh strawberry topping, what's not to like about this dessert pizza? Be creative and add your favorite toppings like kiwi fruit, peach and banana slices and even chocolate curls.

18-oz. tube refrigerated sugar
   cookie dough
8-oz. pkg. cream cheese, softened
2 c. frozen whipped topping,
   thawed

1 t. vanilla extract
1 c. powdered sugar
12-3/4 oz. pkg. strawberry glaze
16-oz. pkg. strawberries, hulled
   and sliced

Roll out dough onto a greased 12" pizza pan; bake according to package directions. Let cool. In a large bowl, blend together cream cheese, whipped topping, vanilla and powdered sugar; spread over crust. Top with glaze and strawberries. Serve immediately, or cover and chill until serving time. Serves 6 to 8.

Cherry Dump Dessert

Tamara Long
Huntsville, AR

My mom first tried this tasty recipe one day when she needed a quick dessert for a church supper. It soon became a family favorite and a potluck standard.

20-oz. can cherry pie filling
8-oz. container frozen whipped
   topping, thawed

8-oz. container sour cream
16-oz. pkg. chocolate chip cookies,
   divided

Stir together pie filling, whipped topping and sour cream in a large serving bowl. Crumble all except 6 cookies; gently fold cookie crumbs into mixture. Arrange reserved cookies on top; chill until ready to serve. Makes 6 to 8 servings.

Strawberry Pizza

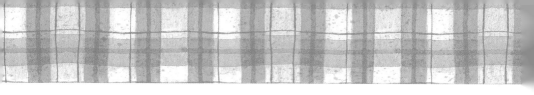

If you're taking a dessert to a potluck or carry-in, secure the lid with a colorful tea towel wrapped around the baking dish and knotted at the top. Tuck a serving spoon inside the knot...ready at at your fingertips!

Instant ice cream social! Alongside pints of ice cream, set out toppings like sliced bananas, peanuts, maraschino cherries, hot fudge and whipped cream. Don't forget the sprinkles!

It's tricky to double or triple recipe ingredients for baked goods like cakes and cookies. Instead, rely on a recipe that feeds a bunch, or prepare several batches of a single recipe until you have the quantity you need.

Turn a favorite cake recipe into cupcakes...terrific for bake sales and neater to serve than slices of cake. Fill greased muffin cups 2/3 full. Bake at the same temperature as in the recipe, but cut the baking time by 1/3 to 1/2. From a cake recipe that makes 2 layers, you'll get 24 to 30 cupcakes.

CAKE

Index

Index

Index

U.S. to Metric Recipe Equivalents

Volume Measurements

1/4 teaspoon	1 mL
1/2 teaspoon	2 mL
1 teaspoon	5 mL
1 tablespoon = 3 teaspoons	15 mL
2 tablespoons = 1 fluid ounce	30 mL
1/4 cup	60 mL
1/3 cup	75 mL
1/2 cup = 4 fluid ounces	125 mL
1 cup = 8 fluid ounces	250 mL
2 cups = 1 pint =16 fluid ounces	500 mL
4 cups = 1 quart	1 L

Weights

1 ounce	30 g
4 ounces	120 g
8 ounces	225 g
16 ounces = 1 pound	450 g

Oven Temperatures

300° F	150° C
325° F	160° C
350° F	180° C
375° F	190° C
400° F	200° C
450° F	230° C

Baking Pan Sizes

Square

8x8x2 inches	2 L = 20x20x5 cm
9x9x2 inches	2.5 L = 23x23x5 cm

Rectangular

13x9x2 inches	3.5 L = 33x23x5 cm

Loaf

9x5x3 inches	2 L = 23x13x7 cm

Round

8x1-1/2 inches	1.2 L = 20x4 cm
9x1-1/2 inches	1.5 L = 23x4 cm